Do you need help with your naming?

Name Review Service. Send us your top name candidates or names in use. We reply with a written opinion and suggestions. One flat rate. Inexpensive. Quick response. Wherever you live, if you have a telephone number or mailing address, we can help. Write, call, or fax for information on this and other naming products and services.

Alder Press
P.O. Box 1503
Portland, OR 97207-1503
Phone: (503) 246-7983
Fax: (503) 452-4265

To order *Names That Sell:*

Mail: Send a check for $14.95 per copy, plus $2.55 shipping and handling, total $17.50, to Alder Press. Please do not send cash. Include your name, address, city, state, ZIP code, phone number, and the book title. Satisfaction guaranteed, or your money back.

Telephone: Credit card users may order toll-free, 24 hours, seven days a week. Call Publishers Group, (800) 858-9055.

Multiple copies: To order copies in quantity or for resale, write, call, or fax for information.

We would like to hear from you.

Your comments and suggestions are always appreciated.

Warning and Disclaimer

Names That Sell

How to Create Great Names for Your Company, Product, or Service

Fred Barrett

Alder Press
1995

To Carol
for everything

Manufactured in the United States of America

Library of Congress Catalog Card Number: 94-079374

Publisher's Cataloging in Publication Data

Barrett, Frederick G.
    Names that sell : how to create great names for your company, product, or service / by Fred Barrett.
        p. cm.
        Includes bibliographical references and index.
        ISBN 0-9636614-7-7

        1. Business names—United States—Popular works.   2. Trade-marks—United States—Popular works.   I. Title.

HD69.B7B37 1994   658.8'27
                                                          QBI94-2198

Alder Press
P.O. Box 1503
Portland, OR 97207-1503 U.S.A.
Phone (503) 246-7983
Fax (503) 452-4265

Contents

The secret to creating great names
is realizing you are not quite there.

PART I - BASICS

I -1
How to Use This Book

Whether you are in a hurry, just want to create one name and get on with it, or wish to study the subject, become proficient in naming, *Names That Sell* is for you. It does not, for the most part, have to be read word for word, from beginning to end. It is set up to be scanned quickly, allowing you to concentrate on what you need and skip the rest. On the other hand, it is a resource book, a keeper, revealing more of itself the more often you read it.

1. Part I - **Basics**. Read this part carefully. *Please*. True, some chapters are more important than others, but, taken as a whole, they impart what do-it-yourself naming is all about.

2. Part II - **Techniques**. This contains twenty-five chapters of naming techniques, each, in turn, suggesting endless variations and combinations. A summary at the beginning lets you decide at a glance whether the technique is of interest.

3. Part III - **Lists**. Containing over 5,000 selected name words, this part makes *Names That Sell* a complete, do-it-yourself book. Add a good dictionary, and you have what you need to start most name-creation projects.

After you have absorbed the above, you are ready to begin creating your great name.

4. The first step is to complete your Project Worksheet, found in Chapter I-20. Here you put your naming project's goals and requirements into writing. Very important.

6. Create your list of name candidates.

7. Narrow your list to the three best.

8. Search the three names for legal availability. Are any owned by someone else? Chapter I-13. Essential.

9. Test your top name or names for marketing quality. What do others think? Do they work? Chapter I-16. The thrust of this book.

10. Follow applicable legal procedures to register and protect your name. Chapter I-12.

11. Begin using your new name.

A great name is forever.
(Until it needs upgrading.)

I - 2
Welcome

We name our children, our tribes, our landmarks and possessions, our enterprises, our creations. These names, if they survive the passage of time, take on what seems to be a life of their own. They strike deep. Would the Arthurian Legends have survived as *Stories of a King*? Sir Lancelot as Joe the Knight? Do you recall Queen Guinevere, Merlin the Magician, and Morgan le Fey? Would the Knights of the Round Table have gained immortality as The Committee?

A few years ago the name Pan Am (Pan American World Airways), and the well-known globe trademark (used since 1928, and a New York City landmark), was purchased at a bankruptcy auction for $1,325,000. The buyer's intent? Not to go into the airline business, but to lease the right to use the name and mark to other airlines, merchandise manufacturers, etc. From the newspaper account:

> Everyone knew what they were trying to get—a brand name that would bring instant recognition around the world that otherwise could take years to build. Eclipse [the buyer, Eclipse Holdings, Inc.] believes it will receive $1,800,000 in licensing fees next year alone.

So Pan Am, in spite of the demise of the airline itself, lives on, a tribute to a great name. Likewise, Stanley Steamer (automobiles), Pony Express (mail delivery), Abercrombie & Fitch (sporting goods), and the *Saturday Evening Post* (magazine), defunct companies, products, or services all, tag along on the back roads of our minds. And sometimes on the "modern freeways," too, as resurrected names, because they were too good to let slip into oblivion.

Just how important is the name you are about to create? How important is the name you are now using, and are perhaps questioning, challenging, reexamining? One answer is a favorite of mine:

Your business name is a million first impressions.

Think of it. Over the course of its existence it will be read, heard, spoken "a million" times. Does it not stand to reason that even a slight upgrade in name quality, multiplied by that number, will pay off?
Pay off to what degree? What kind of money are we talking about? (After all, we are not creating great names for the aesthetic satisfaction they give us.) Coca-Cola is said to value its collection of trademarks at something over one billion dollars. Many other consumer products probably approach that as well; Marlboro cigarettes, Budweiser beer, Tylenol pain reliever. Studies show that the price of a corporation's stock can jump after a name change that Wall Street looks upon favorably. Studies also show that products with good names can be priced higher. *Perrier* bottled water, *No. 5 Chanel, Paris.*
Take the real estate industry's favorite word, "location"—as in location of a business. A bad location, one where complicated directions have to be advertised over and over, will simply wear a business down, to the point where it will often fail. Likewise a name. If you have to keep explaining what exactly you are talking about, what your company does, for instance, if the customer does not "get it," it will wear your business down and wear out your pocketbook. Thus, one of my favorite questions:

Does your name speak to strangers, those not
in the know, outsiders, potential customers?

But many businesses get by with any old name, whatever the grade, you say. True, somewhat. The question then becomes, are they making it *because of*, or *in spite of*, their names? *Names That Sell* assumes its readers wish to do more than just get by.
Names have a long life. If properly used and protected, their lives can be extended indefinitely. Contrast this to patent protection for a product, with a life of seventeen years. But many a product has remained profitable long after its patent protection expired because, among other things, its name was superb.

I - 3
Remarks

Before we begin discussing how to create great names, please allow me a few up-front observations and qualifications.

• Although written to help anyone remotely concerned with English-language business naming, *Names That Sell* assumes you have little or no experience, and attempts to start at the beginning.

• Complete. This book attempts to be a complete do-it-yourself package. But, how complete is complete? As you will discover, name creation is more complicated than perhaps you thought. At what point do details and exotics simply get in the way? There is no perfect answer. What I have attempted to do is present the story in a concise and organized format. I have left out most of my personal naming anecdotes, because, while they are fascinating to me, they tend to drag on and on, taking up more space than their instructional value justifies. Also, I have tried my best to keep *Names That Sell* a genuine how-to book, and not become a book *about* names, their histories, and lore, however fascinating.

• Very important. *Names That Sell* is not just a book about naming new companies, new products, and new services, although one could easily jump to that conclusion. It is aimed equally at long-used names in need of review, reexamination, and perhaps changing, names that were, perhaps, never well thought out in the first place.

• Imprecise as it may seem, the naming of companies, products, and services is lumped together, not treated in separate sections. Why? There is simply too much overlap and duplication to discuss each aspect three times. It is a waste of space. Is McDonald's a business name, a trade name? Yes. Does McDonald's sell products? Many. Is McDonald's a service business? Certainly.

• Abbreviations. Since the phrase "company, product, and service" occurs so frequently throughout the book, it is often abbreviated "CPS." The "C" is a catch-all abbreviation for company, business, professional firm, or nonprofit organization. Since this book is intended for anyone, anywhere, who is interested in creating English-language names, the term "state" should be taken to include like designations where appropriate. *Names That Sell* is sometimes abbreviated *NTS*.

Many trade names and trademarks are used as examples throughout. They are printed without registration marks, such as ®, because they are used only as name word examples—Xerox, rather then Xerox® copiers. Designators, such as Company, Corporation, and Brand, are often omitted to avoid clutter, and to keep the text flowing—Xerox, rather than Xerox Corporation.

• This is obvious, but must be stated. A business name is just that, a name. It is but a small part of the package that makes up the company, product, or service it represents. Also, mention of a particular trade name or trademark is not an endorsement of, or comment on, what it represents. It is for instructional purposes relative to name creation only.

• Another must-be-stated observation. Business names are in that quirky little category—like weather, schools, and restaurants—in which everyone you meet is an expert. Be a little skeptical. Not all opinions are equal. See Chapter I-16, "Testing Your Name."

• This is a book about words. The success of a name, however, also depends upon the skill and consistency with which it is graphically presented (not to mention the number of dollars spent to accomplish it). While we should always keep this in mind when creating our business names, discussion of logos, typefaces, and colors is beyond the scope of this little book. Words, words, words.

• Examples. It seems to me that other books and articles on naming tend to use big-time corporate and brand names almost exclusively for their examples. This is both good and bad. Good, because they have instant recognition and thus instructional value. Why not illustrate with the biggest, the best, the most successful? Bad, because they do not relate to the majority of businesspeople's needs—to create names for small businesses, new products, and services right in their own backyard, so to speak. See Chapter I-4, "Who Are You?" I plead guilty to compulsive name-dropping; it is an occupational hazard. But I have attempted to keep the examples as down-to-earth as possible for the majority of readers.

• Negative examples. A few years ago United Airlines changed its name to Allegis Corporation. It was a stretch, an attempt to create a classy name. It was not, however, well received. After the announcement, an influential shareholder and board member commented acerbically, "It sounds like the next world-class disease." Like the quip that killed the Edsel—"Looks likes an Oldsmobile sucking a lemon"—that was the end of that corporate renaming.

Negative examples in this book are few. This is unfortunate, because there are many mediocre-to-bad real names out there that would be delightfully instructive to pick apart. But prudence requires. Also, it is easy to criticize the work of others (who have their private reasons for what they do). But it is another thing altogether to sit down with pen in hand and create something better.

• In 1865, John B. Stetson introduced his first cowboy hat, calling it the Boss of the Plains. How many hats since then have had names with this kind of appeal? Whatever Mr. Stetson's background, he knew what he was doing. Everyone knows that a company or organization needs a name. *Names That Sell* promotes the idea that almost every product—and service, too!—needs one, even those you would not ordinarily think to name; the difference between another hat and the Boss, between hash and eggs and the Blue Plate Special.

• There is no single, all-purpose road to name creation. Much as I wanted to avoid the shopping list or smorgasbord approach— as it is often an author's cop-out, a fancy way of shortchanging the reader by avoiding the hard work and risk of a well thought out presentation — I had no alternative. The number of naming opportunities is simply too great for a one-formula-fits-all answer.

• Although I firmly believe that any person with a working knowledge of the English language can create great names—in fact, the amateur namesmith has certain advantages, such as knowing his or her business intimately, and operating on the customer's wavelength—I have no control over your time available, personal standards, or level of interest. Plus, the final product, the creation of a truly great name, sometimes involves elements of pure luck or inspiration—serendipity, if you will. No guarantees. Except one: Reading *Names That Sell* and following its precepts, will, I believe, substantially reduce your chances of adopting a bad name. And that is worth a great deal.

Pick flowers. Create names.

I - 4
Who Are You?

Of the approximately ten million American businesses, what kinds do most of you operate—and therefore name? While we are at it, what size business are you most likely to own or work for? A convenient measure is employment. In the fifty states, sixty-five to seventy percent of businesses employ from one to four people. This holds true in both large and small states, rural and urban. Ninety-five percent of all businesses employ under fifty people. At the other extreme, fewer than one percent employ over 500. So we have our answer: the likelihood is that you work in a so-called small business environment.

The United States list below is far from complete, but it will give you a feel for the most common potential naming situations. Franchise-type businesses, such as gasoline service stations, where the owner does not normally name the company. product, or service (CPS), are omitted, as are highly specialized manufacturers, etc. The numbers are for businesses (not numbers of employees) listed in the White Pages and Yellow Pages of phone books. An increasing number of people, however, are working out of their homes. While they may or may not use a business name, many do not show up in statistics because their telephone listing is by personal name only.

After the number, the Standard Industrial Classification Code main category is given, followed, after the dash, by some examples of the largest sub-occupations in the category. Source: American Business Lists, P.O. Box 27347, Omaha, NE 68127.

909,000 Health Services—Physicians, Chiropractors, Optometrists, Psychologists.

799,000 Misc. Retail—Pharmacies, Antiques, Sporting Goods, Jewelers, Gift Shops, Florists, Weddings, Art.

739,000 Wholesalers—Durable Goods.

663,000 Business Services—Advertising Agencies, Copies, Photographers, Computer Consulting, Employment Agencies, Photo Finishing, Interior Decorators.

589,000 Personal Services—Cleaners, Photographers, Beauty and Barber related (344,000), Tax Return Preparers, Weight Control.

516,000 Eating and Drinking Places—Take Out, Catering, and Bars.

499,000 Other Construction Trades—Plumbers, Heating and Air Conditioning, Electrical, Roofing, Excavating.

445,000 Membership Organizations—Trade Organizations, Labor, Clubs, and Churches.

435,000 Legal Services.

404,000 Real Estate—Apartments and Property Management.

381,000 Home Furnishings, Computers, Music.

380,000 Engineering, Accounting, Management Services.

377,000 Automotive—Boats, Recreational Vehicles, Aircraft.

327,000 Wholesalers—Nondurable Goods.

293,000 Miscellaneous Repair Services—Television, Video, Appliances, Jewelry, Upholsterers, Welding, Locksmithing.

285,000 Food Stores—Grocers, Convenience, Bakers.

285,000 Insurance Agents.

274,000 Building Construction—General Contractors.

253,000 Building Materials, Hardware.

248,000 Social Services—Marriage and Family Counselors, Social Services, Child Care.

232,000 Men's and Women's Clothing, Apparel.

159,000 Agricultural Services—Veterinarians, Pet and Horse Related, Landscape and Lawn Maintenance.

151,000 Amusement and Recreation Services.

145,000 Printing and Publishing.

121,000 Motor Freight and Warehousing.

93,000 Hotels, Motels, and Campgrounds.

67,000 Transportation Services—Travel Agencies.

61,000 Financial—Stock Brokers, Financial Consultants.

I - 5
Frequent Naming Mistakes

• **Let's pick a name.** Not taking business names seriously. Waiting till the last minute.

• **What business am I *really* in?** No written statement of naming objectives. No marketing plan for the venture.

• **That's my baby.** Thinking the first name that pops to mind is so brilliant, so original, no one else could possibly have thought of it before.

• **Ego-trip naming.** A higher-level someone gets an inspiration (often his or her own name) and *imposes* it on the company without regard to whether it works or not.

• **Too much "research."** Getting so imbued with the naming styles and trends in a business that one cannot break away from the crowd and create a truly distinctive name.

• **If I build it, they will come.** My company, product, or service is so good (I am so great), if people really want it they will seek me out. So I do not need a marketing plan (which includes a great name) after all.

• **Snubs by snobs.** We do not deign to do business with the unwashed masses—talk to strangers. Therefore, a bland, even obfuscatory, identifier will do nicely, thank you.

• **Too much input by others.** Throwing the naming process open to people who do not have any idea what they are doing.

• **Too little input by others.** Not allowing participation by those who could make a real contribution. Even worse, failure to try the name out on a broad spectrum of real people before adopting it.

I - 6
Marketing in a Nutshell

Football, as someone once said, is really a simple game made complicated. Your team moves the ball toward the opponents' goal and prevents them from reaching yours. Likewise marketing: simple in concept, but complicated.

The First Great Rule of Marketing: Make it easy for your potential customer to say yes.

This is, of course, easier said than done, and is often lost sight of as companies grow. To put the rule into effect requires an exhaustive, step-by-step analysis of every element of even the tiniest business. One element is the name. Your customer has to be able to find you, know what you are about, to remember you, for gosh sake.

The Second Great Rule of Marketing: Repetition. Better a steady, consistent effort, fifty-two weeks of the year, than a big, once-in-a-while splash. A great name is repetition in spades.

The Elements of Marketing: All marketing—the plan and its execution that result in ringing the cash register—revolves around the same basic formula. It does not matter whether you are selling automobiles or ice cream cones, giving poetry readings to publicize your latest anthology, or providing dental services. The elements have been stated by many people, in a variety of ways, but they all boil down to something like this:

1. Attention: Grab your potential customer by the eyeballs with something that will make him or her stop for an instant and want to investigate further. The headline function.

2. Interest: Tell your prospect the benefits of your company, product or service in terms of his or her self interest. Do not confuse this with a mere listing of features.

3. Desire: Create the desire to buy. Often this is accomplished by playing to the basic emotional drives—desire for wealth, pleasure, beauty, acceptance, etc.

4. Close: End with a selling proposition so powerful they cannot resist. Ask for the order.

A great name is an integral part of your marketing plan. To one degree or another it respects all of the above. A bland, pedestrian name merely identifies your company, product, or service. A great name reaches out beyond those already familiar with what your company, product, or service (CPS) is about and speaks to the stranger.

End of marketing lesson. Now to begin naming.

Margaret Mitchell's working title for *Gone with the Wind* was *Tomorrow Is Another Day* (and variations). Scarlett O'Hara's draft name was Pansy.

I - 7
Our Strategy

Separating the experienced namesmith from the beginner, aside from the obvious, is attitude, or outlook. The novice sees a naming project as an over-and-done-with proposition. Someone who has done it many times sees it differently. He realizes that naming, in spite of its seeming permanence, is an ongoing process.

To expect to come up with the perfect name, the ultimate name, every time, given the limited time available for study and creation, is a bit unrealistic. Great names, for the most part, are the result of effort and ongoing evaluation. Even a product name, thought to be more or less frozen and very difficult to change, needs monitoring and evaluation along the way. Always the question: Is it doing the job? Could it be improved upon? To think otherwise is like buying Version 1.0 of a computer software program and doggedly sticking with it as upgrades 2.0, 3.0, 3.1, 4.0, and so forth pass you by. When and how to change a name is discussed in Chapter II-25.

There are many stages and levels of sophistication in name creation. Strangely, sometimes the wheel comes 'round again, as they say. After the time, effort, and money of "higher-level" naming (à la this book) is spent, the name selected can be one casually suggested the first day—"Why don't we call it the Whizbang Deluxe?"—or one somebody's kid thought up at the breakfast table.

That is all right. It is important to go completely through the process (within reason). It is also important to keep your notes. They will help you evaluate your name as time goes by. If a change is deemed necessary, you, or someone else, will not have to go through it all again. Powerful forces, however, descend upon us, suggesting otherwise. Our dominant feelings are to sweep the papers off the table (or delete the computer files) and start over each time from scratch.

Tyro namesmiths are often shocked to discover the number of times their favorite words have been used before, often locked up as registered trademarks, well-known or obscure. This is why I suggest creating first, second, and third choices, not falling in love with your first and one and only. Again, easier said than done. It takes a great deal of perseverance to push on.

Another strategic decision many of us contend with, especially in naming companies, is whether to create a name that gets right to the point, does the job right now—Alec's Coins and Stamps—or a broader-based name to grow into—the Wonderful World of Collectibles—a name you can build upon. See Chapter II-24, "Developing a Theme." The choice is yours, but the slant in *NTS* is to opt for a name that will get things going right now. Because if we do not get our company, product, or service off the ground today, it is academic how well positioned we are for tomorrow.

Another comment on the above. Most names are compromises. One writer describes this compromise as "newness, going hand in hand with a chord of familiarity." Put differently, a great name does not necessarily have to be wild, startling, or "creative." It has to be appropriate, well thought out, and do the job.

I - 8
Elements of a Great Name

What attributes do you seek for your business name? What word or words best describe it —*powerful, exotic, catchy, dignified, whimsical, strong, informative, funny, meaningful, clever, dominant, elegant, outrageous, short, bold, unique, romantic, technical-sounding?*

The following list of elements is something of a checklist, in that you progressively work your way through it. Starting with number one, you add up the number of "tests" your name passes. The first five are basic. Every name should pass them. If it does not, there should be a specific reason. The first five are also the tests for existing names, those created in times past, when, perhaps, little consideration was paid to naming as a marketing device.

A good business name will:

1. Be easy to read, pronounce, and spell.

2. Communicate essential information.

3. Project the appropriate image to the intended audience.

4. Be easy to remember.

5. Be legally available.

For a good name to become a great name, it will:

6. Have a distinctive, inspired quality.

7. Have stood the test of time.

Expanding upon the above:

1. **Read, pronounce, and spell**. Will a stranger, someone seeing or hearing it for the first time, have any trouble with it? Is it easy for a tired, bored telephone operator to say for the five hundredth time late Friday afternoon? Does it pass muster in the warehouse? When your banker presents it to a loan committee, does everyone say, "Huh?" Does it "sound" to a job applicant like a company he or she would be proud to work for, or a product or service they would be proud to sell? How does it sound in a radio commercial when the speaker is talking rapidly, trying to cram everything into thirty seconds? Can it be understood? Most importantly, do potential customers draw a momentary blank, hesitate, then skip over it because it is not worth their while to take the time to figure it out? Walsingham Media Interface Associates? Or AdShop?

2. **Communicate essential information**. Communicate means, among other things, using words within the average person's vocabulary. Diadem Enterprises, Alacrity Software, Paradigm Technology? Sometimes understanding the precise meaning is not that important. It is the sound, the look, the "feel" of the word. Does it contain technical jargon? If so, is it necessary? Ophthalmologist versus eye doctor. See Chapter I-17, "Using the Dictionary," and II-23, "Argot and Jargon."

Essential means, primarily, making it clear what your CPS is about. This is not an obvious element by any means. Take a look in any telephone listing. How many business names convey no clue as to what they do? This may be excusable, unavoidable. The point is, however, to be aware, as there are many exceptions and variations. For instance, with products, the packaging, logo, and slogan can offset the fact that the name itself does not stand alone. If the firm is listed under "Real Estate Appraisers" in the Yellow Pages, you know. But is it always presented so?

3. **Project the appropriate image to the intended audience**. There is more leeway here than one might imagine. A professional firm may opt for a traditional-sounding name emphasizing dignity. Dilingham, Chelsea and Hart. Or, believe it or not, project an image not so

different from a fly-by-night outfit—Willie Johnson's Personal Injury Express Law Firm. Different clientele. Names for toys can vary from the rather formal-sounding Rubik's Cube to Hula Hoop and Barbie doll. Cyclone Fence projects the idea of strength and durability. Eating and drinking establishments seek their customers from a wide spectrum—the Park Lane Tea Room to Fuddruckers restaurants to the Wooden Chicken roadside tavern. See Chapter I-19, "Project Worksheet."

4. **Be easy to remember**. This is essentially what *Names That Sell* is about, so no need to elaborate. Most of the techniques listed in Part II attempt to accomplish this, in one way or another, to one degree or another. We want to nail down that elusive, stick-in-the-mind quality.

5. **Be legally available**. If someone else has established prior rights to the name you wish to adopt you will have to seek another. You want to create the type of name that will maximize your property right potential. And you will want to take steps to protect your rights as you continue to use it. This is discussed in Chapter I-12, "Protection and Infringement."

6. **Have a distinctive, inspired quality**. This is an extension of Element 4, easy to remember, adding bonus points, as it were. It can be achieved in as simple a manner as the fortuitous spelling of a surname—J.C. Penney—or as complex as coining an entirely new word, such as Exxon. Or it can be in between, as in the clever combination name U-Haul. It need not be held to world-class standards either. If the owner of a neighborhood establishment creates a name so powerful that his business becomes *the* place to patronize, then he has created a great name. Again, no need for further elaboration, as this is what the rest of *NTS* is all about.

7. **Have stood the test of time**. It must have staying power. Whether a name is eventually acknowledged as "great" depends upon who you are talking to. But one thing is certain: an owner, creator, or committee cannot declare a name great, especially on the day of creation. It must survive in the marketplace. This, of course, brings all the other business factors—quality, financial muscle, competi-

tion, business acumen, luck, timing—into play. Nevertheless, it must survive to be great.

After years of collecting, creating, and sizing up business names, I have adopted the "on a scale of zero to ten" method of informal ranking. You may wish to do the same. Beware, it is habit forming. Of course, this is all very subjective, but a basic, workable name scores five, passing tests one to five. Score names with bonus points between six and eight. An outstanding name scores nine. And a truly inspired name that has passed the test of time is, what else, a "Perfect 10." For a list of some favorites, scoring, in my opinion, perhaps eight, nine, or ten, see Chapter III-27, "Niche Name Hall of Fame."

A simple name can be an elegant name.

I - 9
Brainstorming

Brainstorming, or "joint ideation," is a specific technique developed by Alex Osborn, the advertising guru, and explained in his 1953 book, *Applied Imagination*. The term eventually, after passing through its fad stage, came into general usage, taking many forms. One of the reasons for its popularity, a great name.

In group brainstorming, participants meet for the sole purpose of producing ideas, solutions to specific problems. The basic rules, according to Mr. Osborn:

1. Criticism is withheld until after the session.

2. "Free-wheel." The "farther out" the idea, the better.

3. Produce ideas in quantity. The more ideas, the greater the chance some will be useable.

4. "Hitchhike." Combine and improve upon the ideas of others as soon as stated.

Many people are more creative when energized by a group than when slogging along alone. They work better playing off the thoughts of others. Person One's contribution sparks an idea in Person Two, who blurts it out immediately, which, in turn, sparks an idea in Person Three, and another from One, and so on. Have an assigned secretary, or tape- record the session.

Brainstorming is only one method of obtaining name ideas. Some think it is a great technique, at least to get started, while others believe it worthless. I am most concerned with *when* in the name- creation process you brainstorm, not necessarily if or how. To explain:

Please attempt to push yourself and your group's creativity before beginning your research. One of the big problems in naming is becoming so swamped with information of all sorts you become confused, and eventually frozen into indecision. It is instinctive to want to plunge into "research" first, find out what everyone else is doing or has done. I happen to believe the opposite is best. Give your imagination a long, hard brainstorming run before you clutter your mind up with bushels of secondhand data.

Circus Circus Enterprises held a contest to name its new Las Vegas hotel and gambling complex shaped like a giant castle. It received 183,415 entries, according to an article in the *Wall Street Journal.*

Obvious names included Camelot, 6,135 entries, and Castle Castle, 2,900, plus off-the-wall gems such as Fools Rush In, Calypso Castle, and Funny Bunny Castle. Names like Came-Slot and Cameloot were clever, but management was not amused. A blue-ribbon panel chose Excalibur, submitted by a mere 268 contestants. When asked how he came up with Excalibur, one of the winners said, "It's the first thing that popped into my head."

I - 10
Who Should Participate?

Broadly speaking, there are four ways to go about naming your CPS:

1. Hire a professional name-creation firm or corporate image consultant. They have everything: skilled, creative people, access to computer databases of all sorts, and the ability to market-test thoroughly. Their services are quite expensive, however, and they are located only in a few major cities. For the most part, their clients are large organizations.

2. Work with your local advertising, public relations, and/or marketing specialist. The name is part of the marketing plan anyway. The advice you get is, however, only as good as the people giving it. Remember, everyone is a names expert. Even professionals' naming skills can range from those of canny old pros, who know what works and what does not, to rank novices posturing behind shiny walnut desks.

3. Some small-business people will skip the above and work only with a graphic designer hired to create a logo, letterhead, business card, and possibly the name too.

4. Others—the majority?—for many reasons, mostly financial, will create their own.

While *NTS* is primarily for the small-business, do-it-yourself namesmith, it would be stupid not to consider the benefits of consulting with others. Aside from their various talents, resources, and experience, they can, in my opinion, make an invaluable additional contribution. They have the ability to "see ourselves as others see us," to more or less quote Robert Burns. This, for more people than care to admit, is extremely difficult to do. We can be too close to it all, wrapped up in our day-to-day trivia, to see, pardon the expression, the big picture. Taking that a step further, it has been my experience that many of those who insist most strenuously that they *can* see things from the other person's point of view are often the very ones who cannot. And that is death in marketing.

Also, you may decide, after reading *NTS* and attempting to create The Great Name, that namesmithing is simply not for you, for any number of reasons. Still, after retaining someone to create it for you, you benefit by being a more knowledgeable client. Please remember, however, there is a difference between being a knowledgeable client and a meddling, second-guessing, know-it-all client. On the other hand, do not be intimidated. Do not allow someone to sell you a name you are not comfortable with. Above all, it has to feel good. You have to be proud to say it out loud. It is your company, product, or service, your future, and your money.

If your banker, accountant, or attorney
thinks the name is jerky, it probably is.

I - 11
Naming Contests

Contests are an extended form of brainstorming. I do not like them, however, because they are too often responsibility evaders, knee-jerk "great ideas" disguising laziness or lack of imagination. I believe the time, effort, and money spent on contests are better focused directly upon the task at hand, creating and testing names themselves.

On the other hand, we cannot deny that some classic names are credited to employee or public naming contests, Wheaties and Land O' Lakes reputedly being two.

Contests, I would submit, are best when the real objective is to publicize a new CPS, such as a sports team, and to generate customer and employee interest and enthusiasm.

And, not to forget, some great names just happened. Scotch brand tape came from an epithet thrown at the "Scotch" bosses at Minnesota Mining and Manufacturing Company, now 3M, for not putting enough tape on the rolls. Cracker Jack is from a popular slang term in the late 1800s. Oh Henry! candy bars got their name from women candy makers calling "Oh Henry" to a local idler who hung around and occasionally helped them carry cartons.

If you must, the basic rule for contests: Make it absolutely clear from the beginning that the contest winner is simply that, a *contest* winner. Although you reserve the right to use the entries, you are under no obligation to actually do so. Perhaps award equal prizes to the ten best entries rather than only one to a first-place winner.

I - 12
Protection and Infringement

As stated in the Warning and Disclaimer, this is not a book on the legalities of trademark protection or infringement. It is important, however, to highlight the basic elements for two reasons: One is obvious. You do not want to adopt a name or trademark owned by someone else, incurring the risk of a painfully expensive lawsuit, and then have to start all over again. The other may not be so obvious. There are many types and degrees of protection accorded names and marks. It is not a simple yes or no issue. Therefore, during the name-creation process you should be aware of what *kinds* of names you are creating and the consequences that flow from these choices. Initially this may not seem important. But, as the years roll by, and the name, and what it represents become successful, you will, in all probability, wish to exclude others from using or imitating it. The more "protectable" the name was in the first place the easier this task will be.

First, some explanation:

Trade Name: The word or words a company uses to identify itself. Sometimes this is referred to as an assumed or fictitious business name. Another common term is "d.b.a." or "doing business as"—as in Amos T. Jones d.b.a. Amos Printing Company.

Corporate Name: If your business is incorporated, it will have a corporate name instead of a trade name. Amos Printing Company, Incorporated, or Amos Printing Corporation.

Trademark or Mark: From the Trademark Act of 1946: "Any word, name, symbol or device, or any combination thereof used by a person, or which a person has a bona fide intention to use in commerce, to identify and distinguish his or her goods including a unique product, from those manufactured or sold by others and to indicate the source of the goods, even if the source is unknown."

When registered with the U.S. Patent and Trademark Office, and only when, the mark can be followed by the ® symbol. If unregistered (common law trademark), or registered at the state level, the ™ symbol may be used. Or, you need not use an indication at all.

Service Mark: Same as a trademark, but identifying a service provided. If federally registered, use ®. If unregistered, or state registered, use ℠.

Registration: Federal registration is with the U.S. Patent and Trademark Office (USPTO), and gives national rights. This applies to trade and service marks only, not trade names. The mark will not be accepted if it is the same or confusingly similar to another registered mark. Refusal of an agency to register a name, unless because of prior registration, does not always mean it cannot be used. On the other hand, a registered name can be challenged.

Trademarks may also be registered in individual states. Beyond precluding others from registering the same mark in the state, it serves as a formal notice of record. The strength of protection varies from state to state.

Names are evaluated for registration along with their specific use, never in the abstract. In other words, if you wish to register a name containing the word "apple," you must specify whether you are naming Apple Computers, the Apple Tree Cafe, or apples grown in Washington state.

A trademark application will be refused if the mark:

1. Does not serve to identify goods or services coming from a particular source.

2. Is immoral, deceptive, or scandalous.

3. Disparages a national symbol.

4. Consists of, or simulates, the flag of the United States, a state, or a foreign nation.

5. Includes the name, portrait, or signature of a living individual without his or her consent, or that of a deceased president of the United States with a living widow, without her consent.

6. Resembles a registered mark in a way that is likely to cause confusion, mistake, or deception.

7. Is merely descriptive or deceptively misdescriptive.

8. Is primarily geographically descriptive or deceptively misdescriptive.

9. Is primarily a surname.

Some advantages of federal registration:

1. The date of application is constructive notice of first use nationally.

2. Gives you the right to sue in federal court, plus other legal advantages. You may be eligible to receive treble damages and attorney fees. Also, criminal penalties for trademark counterfeiting may be available. Because you have given constructive notice, the opposition's "good faith" defense may be eliminated.

3. It is prima facie evidence of the validity of registration, your ownership of the mark, and your exclusive right to use it in commerce.

4. You gain the right to deposit a request with U.S. Customs Service to stop imported, knockoff products bearing your mark. This is very important.

5. A federally registered mark has advantages if you decide to register your mark in foreign countries.

Please note: We are not dealing with **patent** or **copyright**. Many people confuse these terms with trademark, probably because patent and trademark registrations are handled by the same branch of government, the USPTO. Copyright is handled by the Copyright

Office of the Library of Congress and has nothing to do with registering business names, slogans, etc. The rules governing the three are related, however, being known collectively as the law of unfair competition or intellectual property law.

How to register a trademark with the USPTO.

You can retain an attorney to handle everything, or do it yourself. Of course, you or your attorney will have first searched the name for availability. See Chapter I-13. It is a waste of time and money to submit an application for a name that is already registered, or pending registration, when it is so easy to check in advance. You should also have used the mark in interstate commerce, and be able to prove it. Forms can be obtained from the U.S. Department of Commerce, Patent and Trademark Office, Washington, DC 20231.

How to register a trademark with a state.

Most of the state agencies that handle trademarks use the term "Secretary of State," "Corporate Division," or something similar, in the title. It is generally a simple, straightforward, and inexpensive process. As with federal trademark registration, state registration is optional.

The same agencies usually handle corporate name and unincorporated business name (assumed business name) registrations. Unlike trademark registration, you must register these names to do business in the state. It is important to realize that registering a name as a corporate or assumed business name is not a substitute for registering the same name as a trademark, if you plan to use it as such.

As we proceed, we will begin to label names, putting them in different categories. For some this is very subjective. You and I may think a name belongs in a certain category or categories. Our attorney may think differently. A court of law may eventually disagree with all of us.

Also, I must warn you again, trademark law is a complicated specialty. There is no way I can cover every facet, every case, every rule, every exception, even if I were competent to do so. For a lay reader to draw what he or she believes are ironclad conclusions from this brief outline is sheer folly. The reason I belabor this point is I have seen many people do just that, draw legal conclusions from incomplete and inaccurate information. For answers to your specific questions, consult a qualified attorney, most likely a trademark specialist. Also, there are good books on trademarks for the lay reader. A few are mentioned in Chapter IV-2, "Helpful Reading."

If we were to select one word to describe a name that serves its marketing function well, it could be "distinctive." Fortunately, that is the key word on the legal side as well. The more distinctive the word or words used in a name (or mark), the more protection the law will accord. Distinctive names are considered strong names.

The accepted trademark categories, from strongest to weakest:

Arbitrary and **coined** words. Arbitrary words have no meaning relative to the product or service they represent. Apple Computers. Coined words are created just to identify the product or service and have no other meaning. Kodak, Exxon. Both are considered "inherently distinctive" and may be registered when first used. They are also given the broadest scope of protection. See below.

Suggestive words require some thinking or imagination to determine what they describe. Downy fabric softener, Campfire marshmallows, Sani-Flush. Suggestive names are also inherently distinctive.

Descriptive names tell something about the product or service without people having to figure it out. They include surnames (Adams Packing Company), geographic names (Main Street Deli, Southwest Water Systems), laudatory expressions (Super Auto Service), and other words and symbols. They are deemed not inherently distinctive and cannot be registered federally on first use. Sometimes, however, they may be entered in the *Federal Supplemental Trademark Register*, as kind of an on-notice holding area, till they become "distinctive" from continued use (approximately five years) and are granted full rights. This is called acquiring secondary meaning.

Generic words: These words are available to everyone. If you open Ray's Restaurant, you cannot tie up the word "restaurant" for your exclusive use. You cannot register it as a trademark. Every restaurant has the right to describe itself as a restaurant. These are the weakest name words. However, a name deemed generic or merely descriptive in one use may be inherently distinctive in another. Again, the apple example.

Scope of protection. The strongest marks, those inherently distinctive, are accorded broad protection, and can be defended against: 1. The same mark put in use at a later date. 2. A mark that is confusingly similar to the people the mark is intended to influence, so as to cause them to mistake the origin of the product or service. (Note: Creatively altering or misspelling words is not enough to differentiate.) 3. The same or confusingly similar mark used for an entirely different product or service. (McDonald's restaurants sued to stop a motel company from using the name McSleep Inns and won.) 4. Likewise, use in a noncompeting geographic area.

On the other hand, the rights of weak marks, those accorded narrow protection, may be enforced only when the marks are very similar or the same, and used for the same products or services in the same geographic area, etc.

Another point worth mentioning, obvious to some, but perhaps not to others: registering agencies do not step up to defend your rights. It is completely up to the owner to prosecute these rights and pay the costs involved. The type of trademark you create in the first place, date of first use, registration and/or common law usage, and diligence in the use and protection of the mark along the way all compose the package of elements a court will consider.

How does the above affect our specific task at hand, creating a great name?

The dilemma: Often there is a conflict between the type of name desired in a legal-protection sense and one desired in a marketing sense. The strongest types—arbitrary, coined, suggestive—by their very definitions are not descriptive. Therefore they can take much longer, require much more customer education, more advertising, more money, to become established. Once established, however, being distinctive and unique, they have the potential to be much more potent marketing tools, in addition to being protectable. Potential, that is. Just because a name is arbitrary, coined, or suggestive does not necessarily mean it will be a great, or even a good, name.

A descriptive or generic name, or one combining the two, has the opposite effect. It is easily understood from first use, requiring much less time and advertising effort to educate those in the chain of recognition. To create such a name requires less work, imagination, money, and, especially, risk. And "riskless," noncontroversial, descriptive names may be more easily accepted in a committee-type approval process, etc. But competitors can snuggle up to weak names with look-alike, copycat names, hitchhiking on your efforts and goodwill, siphoning off sales dollars that should be yours. And there is little you can do about it, because you do not have a name capable of early or broad protection.

The name Green Giant, 1925, was originally created to describe the "giant" peas inside, not the man we see on the can or package today. The trademark attorney suggested a picture of a giant on the can to make it into a stronger mark. So, a brown-colored, unsmiling giant was adopted. It took ten more years to make him green and friendly.

Alert! This is especially important if you are naming a product or service that is truly innovative, the first one on the market. Here you have an opportunity to create a distinctive and preemptive name that can become very powerful and valuable. You are not only naming your product, you are naming *the* product. Purveyors of "me too" products seldom have this opportunity (and seldom care). I am reminded of the Dustbuster hand-held, cordless vacuum cleaner (a name I will take to be suggestive) and the many, I believe, unsuccessful attempts to create sound-alike names by competitors. I do not know if Dustbuster's manufacturer, Black & Decker, really introduced the first small vacuum of this type, but, with the dominance a great name, they have positioned it as such.

The extreme, of course, is creating a mark that proves so popular, so good, nobody can think of a better descriptive word for it.

Eventually a court may rule it generic: everybody's word. Oh, what a pleasant problem to have. Wouldn't any namesmith like to be credited with creating a name so good it "went generic"?

Some former trademarks that have become generic: *aspirin, brassiere, cellophane, cube steak, dry ice, escalator, kerosene, linoleum, mimeograph, shredded wheat.*

Of course, that is very unlikely today, because most well-known, highly valuable, and commonly misused trademarks are avidly policed and protected. To see which trademarks currently in use are threatened by genericicity, note the print, radio, and television advertisements that stress the word *brand*—"Scotch brand cellophane tape"—or state something like "Jeep is a registered trademark of Chrysler Corporation."

Or peruse the notices in writers', editors', and publishers' magazines. Some marks currently being aggressively protected by educational programs: Kelly® brand temporary help services, Kleenex® tissues, Citibank® financial services, NutraSweet® brand sweeteners, BIC Wite-Out® correction fluids, Weight Watchers® weight loss program, Rollerblade® skates, Day-Glo® fluorescent paints, GORE-TEX® fabrics, Pillsbury Bake-Off® contest, Crayola® crayons, Magic Marker® brand markers, Frigidaire® refrigerators, StairMaster® brand climbers, Sony Walkman® headphone stereos, Weed Eater® brand trimmers, and Jockey® brand underwear.

It is important to use trademarks properly, in speech and writing. For example, Xerox Corporation's notice in *Writer's Digest* politely asks you to "Copy a copy on a Xerox® copier." A trademark should not be used as a verb. Never "Xerox" it. It should always be capitalized, and used as an adjective, followed by a generic noun. "Xerox" identifies one specific brand of copier manufactured by Xerox Corporation only.

I - 13
Searching for Similar Names in Use

You have made your choices, created your top three names. Or maybe you just have a list for consideration. But are they available for your use? At this point, you should conduct a search. Roughly speaking, there are two types:

Do-it-yourself searches: Informal or random searches might be better descriptive terms. Besides identifying duplicate names, which is one of the few clear-cut aspects of any search, informal searches are done to gain a feel for what is out there, how crowded the field is, whether you should move on to something else.

Professional searches: Even professional searches, where you pay a specialist, may not be complete in the sense a novice might imagine. They only cover what is specified, usually marks of record. Common-law trademarks, those in use but not registered, can be searched too, but at additional expense. It is, however, impossible to search every conceivable use of a name in the United States, Canada, and around the world. So it is a matter of where the search stops.

Note, we are only discussing searching the word components of trademarks, not the graphics. As stated earlier, graphics are beyond *NTS*. Also, some of the techniques discussed in this chapter apply only to trade names, and others only to trademarks.

Conducting a do-it-yourself search:

Searching the precise word or words in your chosen name is only the beginning, whether your objective is to register the name or simply avoid infringement. Because registration examiners often consider variations in spelling to be "deceptively similar" and grounds for denial, even an informal search should explore every variation you can think of. Such as:

• Arbitrary or suggestive parts. Alpha tape decks—Alpha

• Phonetic equivalents. Easy—easi, ez, e z, eezee, etc.

• Other likely endings. Track—traq, trak, trax

• Singular and plural. Cougar—cougars

• Separate element and syllables. SkiJock—ski, jock

• Phonetic equivalents and plurals. Smartloc—smart lock, smart lox, smart loq, smart locs

• Separate parts of combination names. TacoMan—taco, man

• Double and single consonants. Fox—Foxx

• Translations of foreign words. *Abogado*—attorney

• Numeric variations; Arabic, roman, and literal. 2, II, two

• Confusingly similar. 2000—2001, 2010, 200

• Imaginative variations. Water chem—H^2O Chem

Telephone directories. This is the starting point, especially for trade names. Check your local business listings for every variation you can think of. Then check every pertinent heading in the Yellow Pages. If you live in a small town or rural area, by all means check the directory of the main metropolitan area in your state. Beyond that, I find it helpful to explore the directories of major cities throughout the country, both for ideas and search purposes. If, for instance, you are naming an eating or drinking establishment, look in places where the competition is very intense—New York, Los Angeles, Dallas, Seattle, Chicago—because commercial competition spawns name competition.

If you wish to go further, you can buy the trade names of every U.S. business listed in the White or Yellow Pages on CD-ROM. Produced

by American Business Lists of Omaha, Nebraska, (402) 331-7169, it
is inexpensive, and available at your computer software store.

Trade publications. Checking these is a must if you are naming a
product or service. The problem: they are often obscure magazines,
not found in libraries. Retrieval systems are not much use either,
because they do not include the advertisements, which are mostly
what we are interested in. If you do not subscribe, or have a friend in
the business, try this: Visit outfits in the business. Commonly, older
issues of trade magazines are used for waiting room reading, and are
yours for the asking.

Libraries. There is no standardized search method. What is
available depends upon the size and quality of the library you visit. If
you live in a small town, it may very well be worth a trip to the big city
or a large university. Beyond a good collection of national and
international telephone directories, a large library will have a business department with an astounding number of special topic directories.

Larger libraries will most likely subscribe to the *Official Gazette—
Patent and Trademark*, the weekly publication of the USPTO. The
problem: The amount of data is so vast, with hundreds of new
trademarks approved, applied for, and abandoned each week, that it
is almost impossible to read them all. And they go back over fifty
years. There must be a better way. And there is:

Patent and Trademark Depository Libraries. This is a national
network of libraries with special sections to serve inventors, patent
and trademark attorneys, and businesspeople like you. The reason
they are so innovative and important is, prior to their establishment
(and computerization of the patent system) the only complete collection of patents available to the public was at the USPTO. (The *Official
Gazette* prints only abstracts.) One had to hire a searcher, write, or
travel to Washington, D.C., to obtain copies.

To date there are about seventy Depository Libraries in forty-six
states, some in city libraries, others at major universities. California,
Florida, and Ohio, have four each, the maximum per state at present.
Depository Libraries may, in turn, be linked with affiliate libraries

around a state, on-line, or in other ways. For more information, contact: Office of Patent Depository Library Programs, Crystal Mall 2, Room 306, USPTO, Washington, DC 20231, (703) 557-9686.

As with standard libraries, not all Depository Libraries are equal. The newer ones may be building their collections, which are expensive, and may be computerized to a lesser degree.

Fortunately, trademarks are easily searched at well-stocked Depository Libraries. The Trademark Register is contained on CD-ROM (CASSIS), and is updated every few months. You can learn to operate the computer in a few minutes. How thoroughly you search, as discussed above, is another matter. Just because you have gone directly to the source, do not walk off thinking you have it covered. For instance, you should also check *Official Gazette* issues after the date of the CD-ROM. Be sure to ask for help and suggestions from the library staff.

Searching with a personal computer modem. If you subscribe to CompuServe, you can access the latest registered trademarks from your office or home. The lists include both federal and state registries. Contrasted to searching at a Depository Library, it is more convenient, but more expensive, as Trademark Register searching is not a service included in the basic monthly package. They charge for each report. And if you make a mistake, you pay anyway. For CompuServe information, call (800) 848-8990. Sorry to harp on this, but just because you are using a computer does not mean you are performing a professional search.

There are other on-line databases, each with advantages and disadvantages in ease of use, price, method and thoroughness of search. Dialog, (800) 334-2564, and IntelliGate, (800) 543-8843, are two. Detailed information is not given here because I have not used every one and it gets out of date so quickly. If you are comfortable with computers and feel you will use a service enough to justify its cost, calling the three numbers listed is all you need to get started.

State secretary of state offices and departments of commerce. The department will have a number of lists of names registered. Some states register for the entire state, others only the county or counties where business is conducted.

Each state has lists of corporations, partnerships, assumed business names, and, if the state registers them, trade and service marks. You can visit the office, telephone, or, probably in some states, fax or connect directly on-line. This is all public information, to the point where the states do a nice business selling the various lists.

While we are discussing state registration, please note that a decision to accept or reject is not always clear-cut. If your name is turned down, it may just be the opinion of the first examiner who reviews it. If rejected because of similarity, rather than priority of an exact name, the decision may be appealable. Find out what the appeal process is. At a minimum, ask to talk with a supervisor to find out the reason your name was turned down. If this is really the name you want, far better than number two or three on your list, it may be worth a face-to-face meeting rather than a telephone conversation. Or, you may wish to retain an attorney. He or she may be able to negotiate an acceptable compromise.

Professional searching:

Going direct. Many professional trademark searchers advertise in the Yellow Pages of major cities. Look under the heading "Trademark Agents & Consultants." If your directory does not have that heading, or something similar, try "Patent Searchers," as some firms do both.

A simple call to the 800 number will get you the firm's guidelines and prices. If you want a more complete list than found in your local book, consult the Washington, D.C. or New York City telephone directories. One search firm, the one providing the on-line service to CompuServe, called Compu-Mark, is Thompson and Thompson of North Quincy, Massachusetts. Phone (800) 692-8833.

Hiring a trademark attorney. In the old days, attorneys had "associate" searchers who "lived" at the Patent Office, prowling the stacks, making photocopies of the dog-eared patent and trademark originals therein. Today, law offices can search on-line themselves, but may use the old guys, who can do it on-line, as well. The cost will be considerably more than going direct to a searcher, but you get more. Among other things, you buy the attorney's professional opinion on how the report should be interpreted and what to do about it. Sometimes the report's message is clear-cut: the name is taken, and it cannot be registered. Other times the situation may be hazy. What you do will be determined by your circumstances and your attorney's advice.

Summary. The suggestions above do not pretend to cover every method and variation. That is not the purpose of *NTS*. Maybe the purpose is to discourage you a bit, by making you aware of your limitations. In any event, approach searching logically. Before you go running to your attorney with every name you like, conduct some do-it-yourself searching as outlined above. It is embarrassing to have the attorney find "your" name already listed in the Yellow Pages.

Simultaneous with searching, you should have started your basic testing. Chapter I-16. What is the point of getting serious about a name that will eventually flunk the marketing tests? I know this sounds like a circular rat race, but one should not be done to the exclusion of the other. Do your homework before you waste your attorney's time and your money.

If your financial backers don't like it, don't use it.

I - 14
Identifying Your Lookup Word

What is the most universal word describing what your company, product, or service is about, the one most people would think of first? Under what listing would someone look in the Yellow Pages? This is what I refer to as your lookup word.

For instance, you are opening a shop specializing in repairing and rebuilding computer hard drives. Your primary Yellow Page lookup word is Computers. The secondary word would be Repairs (more accurately, Computers-Service & Repair). Other lookup words might be Hard Disks or Hard Drives.

Or, you are naming a new eatery, serving exotic pastries and gourmet coffee. The lookup word appears to be Restaurants. Under the specialty sublistings, we have Coffee Houses and Desserts. Or is it Coffee & Tea - Retail, which includes many shops with similar fare?

Whether you incorporate your lookup word or words into your name is another issue. On one hand, naming your business Computer Hard Drive Repair Company is accurate. But it is also descriptive, and full of generic words, offering very limited protection (except, perhaps, as a local d.b.a.). Of 360 listings under Computers - Dealers, or Computers - Service & Repair, in my local Yellow Pages, about ten percent use all or part of *Computer* as the first word in their name.

Under Coffee & Tea - Retail, twenty-five percent of 112 establishment names use Coffee or a variation, Caffe or Kaffee, as the first word. This follows, for it is more of an impulse, convenience product/ service.

Interestingly, the largest chain by far, with dozens of shops, is Seattle-based Starbucks Coffee. Starbuck, a character in the novel *Moby Dick*, was a coffee-loving sailor. Choice of his name aptly illustrates, in my opinion, what appropriate naming is all about.

When you have identified your lookup word, or words, list them, most inclusive first, on your Project Worksheet, discussed in Chapter I-20.

I - 15
The Yellow Pages

When their fingers go walking, will they stop at your name? For many businesses, this is a critical question.

Having identified your lookup words, the next question is, are you a Yellow Pages lookup business?

• Are there many competing, quarter-, half-, or full-page advertisements under your heading?

• Do customers call you in an emergency—towing, plumbing?

• Are you patronized so infrequently some people do not remember your business name from visit to visit, no sense of continuity—florists, travel agents, and professionals, in some cases.

If you answered yes, then you are likely a Yellow Pages lookup business.

What is the formula for a successful Yellow Pages ad?

The Yellow Pages people will tell you the larger the display ad, plus color, photographs, etc., the more successful your ad will be.

For example: In the Portland, Oregon, Yellow Pages—metro area population one million—the Attorneys heading covers eighty-four pages, and includes eighteen full-page displays, fifty-four partial-page displays, 440 in-column displays, 105 photographs, and many advertisements of both types with color. One attorney has his face in eight different subheading advertisements.

The results of one study, as told in *Advertising in the Yellow Pages*, by W.F. Wagner, showed that for every ten calls received, the display advertisements produced seven, the in-columns two, and a bold-type listing one. (The test company was in a prime lookup business.)

While I agree that displays are more effective, whether they are more cost effective is another matter. If your business has an important degree of differentiation, such as location, often an in-column display can be highly cost effective. Another advantage of an in-column advertisement is you have a degree of control over where it will appear, because it is listed alphabetically. Displays are printed in order of descending size and seniority.

What about the name itself? Here are some suggestions for listing in the alphabetical White Pages, in in-column Yellow Pages, and, to a lesser extent, in Yellow Pages displays:

• Consider including a tag line. Give your reader something to distinguish you from everyone else, a reason to select your business instead of the next one. I think this may be as important as bold type. It can be a simple statement—Barnes & Noble, Booksellers since 1873; your name and slogan—Friedman Bag Co., Our quality is in the bag; or an extended name—Tony Roma's A Place For Ribs.

• I believe it is important to include your address. If just a phone number is given, I often hesitate to call. It strikes me as incomplete. Are they hiding something? How about you?

Sometimes I select a business in the Yellow Pages for locational convenience only. Often, even if a simple phone call will do, I will travel to the establishment to meet the people and evaluate it on the spot. (Perhaps this comes from my years leasing commercial and industrial real estate. Even though my customers mostly came to me—you cannot move the buildings—I almost always made up excuses to visit them in their home environment as well. I felt I learned a great deal.)

Some say listing a post office box number is as bad as nothing at all, projecting a fly-by-night image. And they have a point. I think, however, this may be a little outdated. I have used one for years, and many giant business do the same. One more thing: if possible, include your ZIP code, another small step in making it easier for potential customers, strangers, to find you, and ultimately say yes.

• Another important consideration in winning the battle of the Yellow Pages jungle is, how far down the alphabetical listings a person will look. There are many views on this, but it stands to reason there will be a falloff if the listing is long. You know from your own experience. This brings up the frenzied competition to be first in line. Thus we have AAA Plumbing Company, upstaged by AAAA Action Plumbers, Inc., leapfrogged by AAAAAAAAH Some Plumbing, and so on. These strike the namesmith as being rather crude. But they must work, so we cannot dismiss them out of hand. I would urge, however, to try for something better. The above may have very little going for them except being high on the list.

My experience as a user and advertiser is—depending upon the length of the listing—people will usually read carefully down to at least "C" or "D." (Also, some people will attempt to ignore the screaming displays, feeling they "do not want to pay for them.") People like to shop around a little, not "buy" at the first place they "visit." But not too much, as attention spans soon expire. After that, they are "ready to buy," as the automobile dealers say.

A technique to move to the top of the list:

If, for instance, your name is Gabriel Zoltan, and you do business as Zoltan Plumbing, Inc., add another listing as A Zoltan Plumbing, Inc. (Not A. Zoltan, as it would be listed as Zoltan, A.) You would continue to use the old listing under "Z." (A variation would be to start over from scratch and create a better marketing name.) You would continue to list under the old name, or perhaps change slightly to Zoltan, Gabriel, Plumber. (Different telephone companies may have different rules concerning this practice, and some may not accept such listings. Also, be sure to check your state assumed business names regulations.) I did spot Cherry Street Deli moving up from 241st to second place by becoming A Cherry Street Deli.

• Finally, back to a recurring theme. One of the reasons for paying attention to all these seemingly trivial aspects of business names is that you and your associates perceive them very differently than do your customers, especially Yellow Pages lookers, who are in a big hurry. To you, your name or names are very clear and distinct, because you work with them every day. They are important to you. To your customers, past, present, future, they can be very hazy, and soon forgotten, just like a telephone number once dialed. In many cases, there is little reason for him or her to exert the effort to remember. So they do not. For that matter, how many times do we forget names we specifically *want* to remember, because we were satisfied and want to become repeat customers? But still the name slips away.

Impressive-Sounding Words

Balanced, capability, compatible, concept, contingency, critical, developmental, digital, flexibility, functional, generational, global, hardware, incremental, integrated, international, logistical, management, mobility, monitored, multi, optional, organizational, parallel, policy, programming, projection, quadrant, quantum, reciprocal, responsive, synchronized, systematized, third-generation, time-phase, total, transitional, vertex. Source: *Time* magazine, Sept. 13, 1968, and various.

I - 16
Testing Your Name

Testing your name before you start using it is essential, a must. I am referring, of course, to testing its marketing effect, the very essence of *Names That Sell*. As with the search for legal availability, better to find out beforehand than after. I will not take the space to relate the stories about a few of my name creations that have embarrassed me to tears, because I started using them before testing them out in the big world (however, page 87). Please take my word for it, names that delight you and your creation group can draw blank looks, rolled eyes, even snickers, from the proverbial man in the street when he hears them for the first time. I might add, there is a strong impulse to skip this phase, to get on with it. Do not succumb to this urge.

As with searches, there are both do-it-yourself and professional methods. Since this is a do-it-yourself book, I will only suggest a few simple informal methods. After using a few, your own circumstances and imagination can take over.

Like the pursuit of the ideal name, the time you can spend testing is potentially endless. How many people you contact, and how complicated a plan you devise, is up to you. But the point is to do *something.*

True, your testing pools are not likely to be truly representative groups. Your questions, presumably, are not going to be sophisticated. You are not a statistical expert. Nor are you trained to interpret test data. But you do have a very good chance of uncovering any glaring deficiencies that simply did not occur to you during the creation phase.

Expert or not, remember, you are in control. You do not have to take everything people say at face value. Size up every response situation with a skeptical, but fair, eye. If you feel the response was ill-considered or frivolous, do not hesitate to disregard it; as in sports judging, or a bidding process, where you throw out the highest and lowest scores. On the other hand, make sure you are not massaging the data to make it come out the way you want it to.

How to test:

Validate the elements. The names have passed the basic tests in your opinion, or they would not have gotten this far. What do the intended recipients — customers, associates, and strangers — think of it? To review:

A good business name will:

1. Be easy to read, pronounce, and spell.

2. Communicate essential information.

3. Project the appropriate image to the intended audience.

4. Be easy to remember.

5. Be legally available.

For a good name to become a great name, it will:

6. Have a distinctive, inspired quality.

7. Have stood the test of time.

Preliminary tests:

Mark where your name will appear in the White and Yellow Pages. True, you have generally established this by the first letter, but the idea is to eliminate as many rude surprises as you can. Do not imagine where; mark exactly. Is it convenient for your customers?

Double check name length. A database may accept names up to, say, thirty-five letters, but in most cases that would be too long for marketing purposes. If your name must be long, make sure the meaningful words, the lookup words, occur at the beginning. For example, "Blank Foundation and Hall of Fame" takes up thirty-three spaces. "National Foundation and Hall of Fame of Blank" takes up forty-five. The meaningful "Blank" could be chopped off. I have no absolute maximum number to give you. It depends upon your situation. One expert, however, insists upon a maximum of seventeen letters. See also Chapter II-15, "Naming Nonprofit Organizations."

Test the ratio of words to syllables. Standard writing contains about 1.5 syllables per word. The higher the ratio, the more difficult the reading level. This may be a little too strict for names, but it is a good place to start. What it comes down to is this: if you name has more than one three- or four-syllable word, take a good hard look. Is the word really necessary? "Blank Foundation and Hall of Fame" looks like a mouthful, but has only six words and eight syllables, a ratio of 1.3. International Business Machines has a ratio of 3.0, thus forcing the abbreviation, IBM.

Apply the hard-soft alphabet test.

A	SOFT	N		soft
B HARD		O		SOFT
C hard/soft		P HARD		
D HARD		Q HARD		
E	SOFT	R HARD		
F hard		S hard/soft		
G hard/soft		T hard/soft		
H hard/soft		U		SOFT
I	SOFT	V hard		
J HARD		W		soft
K HARD		X HARD		
L	soft	Y		soft
M	soft	Z hard		

This is my version of the hard and soft sounds of the alphabet. Vowels are given an extra soft "SOFT" designation. Particularly hard-sounding letters, the stop consonants, are "HARD." If you disagree, feel free to make up your own list.

Test your names by noting the hard or soft sound of the first and last letters of each word. The first and very last letters are not of great concern; that would be getting too picky. We are concerned with situations where the ending letter of one word and the beginning letter of the next word create a difficult pause, namely by juxtaposing two hards. Art Trek. This, in my opinion, ruins the flow, melodious sound, the euphony of a name (if, in fact, it had any to begin with). Back to our previous example:

```
International  Business  Machines

S             s H      s s      s
```

The softness of the sounds help to offset the high syllable ratio. The initials, IBM, carry over the pleasant S-H-s sound.

Should your name test out with an H-H, H-h, h-H, or h-h combination, it may be what you want. Some feel an abrupt pause commands attention and respect, making people stop and take notice (akin to a pronounceable middle name, to be discussed in Chapter II-1). Whatever your view, if you have a Hard-Hard situation, say it aloud before you settle on it. Then have others do the same, as part of your testing program. Personally, Hard-Hard names grate on me. When I see or hear one, I say to myself, this guy did not think it through. I score it on the scale of zero to ten accordingly.

Alert! As above, say *every* name out loud a number of times. Listen to others speak it. Test your name for aural quality as well as visual quality. Is it pleasing to the ear? Not doing this is probably one of the biggest mistakes in naming.

Anticipate all shortened versions of the name. Can they be twisted into something derogatory, such as an embarrassing acronym? What abbreviations, initials, and nicknames spring to mind? Ries and Trout, in *Positioning: The Battle for Your Mind*, assert that any name over three syllables is a candidate for abbreviation. But, if equal in phonetic length, people will use the word, not the initials. There is no need, they say, to abbreviate Ford, but General Motors becomes GM.

Testing in the big world:

Simply put, conduct an informal opinion survey. The essential rule
is to keep your questions simple and be a good listener. Questions
should be self-explanatory. If you are in direct contact with the
respondent, take off your "advocate" hat and don your "recorder" hat.
You want the person's first, unencumbered impression. Then, you
might explain a little more — such as, we are naming a new real estate
company, an innovative bicycle lock, or whatever—to get a second
impression. Then shut up. I put this crudely because this is almost
impossible for some people to do. They feel compelled to talk on and
on, really putting words and answers in the respondents' mouths, and,
of course, creating misleading results. You are not a pro at this, and
not after a lengthy analysis. The issue is whether the name works
quickly, with basically uninterested people. Listen to the response,
thank the person, say good-bye, and let him or her go.

What to ask:

Limit to one or two questions. One might be, "What does this name
tell you?" Another, "Do you like this as a name for a Blank?" Or,
"Do you have any comments?" Another might be, "Which of these
three names for a Blank do you prefer?"

A few do-it-yourself suggestions:

Focus groups. This is the trendy term for a bunch of people you
collect to answer questions and express opinions, the passive end, I
guess, of brainstorming. I would prefer to question people individually, but opinions are opinions; we get them any way we can.
    Either way, I would suggest presenting them with the questions in
writing, with simple instructions and check-off boxes. This seems to
be a friendly, nonthreatening approach. If you belong to one, a club
or business association meeting is a great time to hand out surveys.
Just collect them after the meeting.

The telephone test. Make a list of people whose opinions you respect, preferably those with an understanding of your CPS, but not relatives, employees, etc.—people inclined to tell you what they think you want to hear. Call and tell them you are naming your new such and such. In this case, answer any questions they ask. Then go on to any personal conversation you like. Call them the next day and ask what the name was. If a goodly number remember, you are most likely way ahead of the game.

The mail and/or fax test. Mail or fax a questionnaire to individuals or offices. It could read something like: "We are surveying people like you to find the best name for our new Blank. Please post this on your office bulletin board or answer yourself. Check the name you prefer or suggest one. Please return by XX date. Thank you." Sign your name so people will not take it as a joke.

A number of titles for this book were tested by the focus group and the mail and/or fax methods. Although, during the course of writing, I had used over one hundred working titles—some for seconds, some for years—the one I finally settled upon, and really liked, was not selected by a single respondent out of over one hundred people and organizations polled.

A few tips: When mailing a survey, include a stamped, self-addressed envelope. Popular as fax machines are, "snail mail" has not been displaced. I included an incentive to respond, a promise to draw five names from those who responded and send them a free copy of the book. People are flattered when asked for their opinions, but a reward is nice too. Although the title, *Names That Sell*, came out of this survey, and other sources, the test results were not absolutely clear-cut. I could continue creating, refining, and testing forever. Like the name you will create for your company, product (which a book is), or service, I am still on the prowl for the elusive Perfect 10.

The shopping mall or street corner test. This is, of course, difficult for many of us to do. Unless we are professional pollsters or petition signature gatherers, few of us like to approach people cold. The advantages for the do-it-yourselfer, however, are many—great numbers of people, a wide cross section, and quick results. The key is to keep the questions very simple and short. And, if you conduct it on private property, obtain permission from the owner first.

I - 17
Using the Dictionary

Get an up-to-date dictionary. If yours is a hand-me-down relic, please buy or borrow a new one before you begin your tour as a namesmith.

I use the *American Heritage College Dictionary*, Third Edition, 1993. I am not, however, saying it is the best. Everyone has slightly different requirements, hence their own favorites. Also, I guess I am admitting Noah Webster's name does not have to be in the title. Although, as far as naming is concerned, it is a grand testimony to the selling power of a name, since his first dictionary was published in 1828.

With 200,000 words, *American Heritage* is complete enough for my purposes. It is also small and light enough to actually be used, as opposed to the heavier, more impressive ones that, for the most part, are not. As namesmiths our task is to communicate the message to a broad spectrum of people in a clear, concise, and memorable way; at the least, strike a chord of recognition. It is not to show how smart we are, or to try to snow people with a crossword puzzle fanatic's vocabulary.

Many people consider dictionaries dull tomes, to be used only when absolutely necessary, opened quickly, then slammed shut immediately after finding what they seek. Modern dictionaries are different, very user (pardon) friendly. Each time I open *American Heritage*, I find myself seduced into lingering, browsing, prowling around. Maybe the subtitle should be *The Joy of Dix*.

The electronic version of the *American Heritage Dictionary* will be discussed in Chapter I-19.

This is how *American Heritage* is arranged:

1. The standard format: word, pronunciation, variations, and endings.

2. Noun forms and meanings. Most important for namesmiths.

3. Verb forms and meanings. Sometimes useful.

4. Etymology. (Earlier forms of the word.) Note these words, printed in italics, carefully and say them aloud. Write down those that please your eye and ear. There are two reasons for this: One of them could become your sought-after name. Or a word may contain a morpheme (word part) with which to build a coined or combination name. Patience. This is not as onerous as it seems.

5. Idioms. (Phrases in common usage, the meaning of which cannot be derived from the definitions of the individual words.) For example, *freeze* lists the idiom "to freeze in (one's) tracks." *Spot* lists "on the spot."

7. Synonyms. Lists most synonyms for the word, together with brief definitions, so you can compare fine distinctions.

8. Usage panel. Expert opinion on difficult words.

Let me toss in another reason to keep an up-to-date dictionary close at hand. It is obvious, of course, but must be stated. You must check *all* definitions of *every* word you select for use in your names. A secondary meaning may render a seemingly fine name word undesirable, unacceptable.

For example: *Seminal* means "having the power to originate; creative." Very nice. But, it also means "containing semen or seed." Risky. *Savant* means "a learned scholar." I could see many uses for this noble-sounding word, derived from the French *savoir*, to know. But the term *idiot savant* comes so readily to mind (especially after the movie *Rain Man*), that it is most likely a hands-off word. Too bad for Savant Software Systems, etc.

Consider *mistral*, a cold, dry wind that blows through southern France. It also names a windsurfing sail maker. Did they select it simply because it names *a* wind? Did they seek to suggest overcoming adversity by sail and sailor? Was it such a beautiful sounding "wind" word the meaning was considered irrelevant? All of the above? None of the above? The wind word *sirocco* would raise some of the same questions.

I - 18
Practice Exercise

The assignment: Create a name for a new, national, on-line database which will contain the vast body of American legal references.

You may stop here and plunge into your dictionary. Or you may trace through my solution, then make your own contributions and come to your own conclusions.

First, I write down every key word I can think of. I have to start somewhere. I look up each one in the dictionary, reading everything it says about the word. I write down each interesting word I find, even in secondary meanings; every one that, in my opinion, gets at what I am trying to express. I say each word aloud.

Next, I highlight the most promising words on the list, and look up their definitions. And so on. What you will be doing, when you repeat this exercise in your own way, is reading the dictionary perhaps more carefully than you have ever done before, scouring the deep recesses, searching for nuggets and gems, even broken pieces.

1. Some key words to that come easily to mind are: *law, legal, library, book, word, reference, dictionary.* Looking them up, we expand our word list to include the following:

Law: rule, jurisprudence, principle, code, litigate. [Middle English < Old English, *lagu.*]

Legal: statutory. [Middle English < Old French < Latin, *legalis* < *lex*, law.]

Library: reference, collection, data. [Middle English, *librarie.* Latin, *libraria. Liber*, book.]

Book: literary, volume, record, libretto, script, rules, source.

Word: communicate, remark, comment, discourse, talk, speech, promise, command, order, password, watchword, news. Idioms: good word, in a word. *Loquacious*, many words. *Laconic*, few words.

Scanning the nearby, related words (as I should), I come upon:

Word book: lexicon, vocabulary, dictionary.

Reference: meaning, denotation, note, passage, source, mark.

Dictionary: reference. [Middle Latin, *dictionarium.* Latin, *dictio, diction.*]

2. From the above, I narrow the list to the most promising: *jurisprudence, lex, data, record, source, lexicon, mark.*

Jurisprudence: [Latin, *jurisprudencia*: *jus*, law + *prudentia*, knowledge.]

Lex: leges, plural.

Data: datum, singular.

Record: nothing more of interest

Source: same

Lexicon: [L. Greek, *lexikon* < Greek, *lexikos*, of words < *lexis*, word < *legein*, to speak.]

Mark: Mark of quality.

3. Preliminary conclusions. The word *source*, although a great prospect, should have been excluded, because it has been used before. *Data* is overused, but could be used in combination. *Jurisprudence* is too long, but *juris* has potential, although they both have been used many times, and in many ways. Combinations could be made from the short words and word parts: *lex, lexis, ref, data, mark, jur.*

As you may know, we are discussing a real trademark, a real product—Lexis. (Distinguish from Lexus, the automobile.) Was the name found in this, albeit simplified, manner? I really do not know, but it could have been.

Lexis is a gem. It is a one-word name, which I consider a plus, with balance, five letters, and two syllables. It is pronounceable, memorable, and fits nicely on a computer screen and in a logo. As with many Latin words, it has a familiar, yet not-so-familiar, ring to it. And the morpheme *lex* means law, a handy bonus. Loosely interpreted, the name could mean "word of law," which is exactly what the service is about. In my opinion, Lexis is a preemptory trademark, almost impossible to improve upon.

A great name never goes on vacation, never sleeps,
never goofs off, and never asks for a raise.

I - 19
Computer-Assisted Name Creation

While a computer is not essential to name creation, it can be very helpful. And, thankfully, not all computerized assistance is expensive or hard to use.

Perhaps the simplest tool (after the spell checker) is the thesaurus, included with most word-processing programs. Using it is simple and fast, a great way to collect words and word parts to begin building name possibilities. An especially nice feature, at least in the program I use, WordPerfect for Windows, is the ability to click on any secondary word and immediately see the thesaurus entry for it, and so on.

The next level would be the electronic dictionary. As mentioned, I use the *American Heritage College Dictionary*. I also use the *American Heritage III* electronic dictionary, which is available in DOS, Windows, and Macintosh formats. It is advertised at 100,000 words, not the 200,000 words the print edition lists. WordStar Writing Tools Group, (800) 845-1925. (Another, *Random House Webster's College* electronic dictionary, advertises 180,000 words.)

It is a wonderful tool, in my opinion, especially for namesmiths, but does not eliminate the need for the print version. The ability to scan the real page for any related information you might find is too important a feature to give up, in spite of the "browse" function the electronic provides. The electronic version, by the way, costs two to three times as much as the book. You may be able to use it free, however, with your local library's on-line catalog.

Disadvantages of electronic dictionaries: They take up six to fifteen megabytes of space on your hard disk. They are not portable, unless your computer is. To use conveniently, they require a very fast computer. Mine is not fast enough to activate the electronic dictionary each time I wish to look up a single word. It is faster to use the book.

Advantages: You can access while running the major word-processing programs—WordPerfect, Microsoft Word, and Ami Pro. To use the dictionary you do not even have to know how a word is spelled. The program assists you. And the definitions are the same as in the book, not abridged versions. The standard *American Heritage* electronic dictionary does not, however, include extras such as biographical and geographical entries. They are included in the fifteen-megabyte deluxe edition.

Features: Of particular importance to namesmiths is the WordHunter, or word-searching feature. This searches the entire dictionary for every definition that mentions your chosen search word. (Do not confuse this with a thesaurus function, which only lists synonyms and antonyms.) Use this when you seek quantity—lists of idea words.

For example, horse-related words have been used many times, in, or as, business names. By WordHunting *horse*, one finds 296 entries, which can be scanned with the mouse—from appaloosa to bronco, colt, dark horse, maverick, mustang, Pegasus, seahorse, stallion, Trojan horse, and workhorse, plus words related to gear, lore, and more. Hunting another word, *tree*, results in 182 words, from African tulip tree to willow. If you specify *tree OR trees,* you expand the list to 329. The reason: some definitions just happen to use the plural form only. Spruce, for instance, does not appear in the first list.

The narrow, or quality, side of WordHunter allows you to find single "lost" words, those you cannot remember, or never knew in the first place. The example they give is *tea* and *boil*, resulting in *samovar*.

Another feature is called the Wild Card function. You enter part of a word, then insert question marks or asterisks as "wild cards." The program then fills in the wild cards with every real word combination it can "think up." This is useful, for instance, in creating alliterative and rhyming names, discussed in Chapter II-11. The entry dr*, for instance, results in a list of 577 words of all lengths: drab, dragster, dreamland, drifter, drive-in, drizzle, etc. By using question marks, you limit the search to words of a specific length. Dr??? results in only 48 five-letter words: dream, drift, drive, etc.

NamePro name development software

If you would like to take computerized naming a giant step beyond the methods previously suggested, consider a new program called NamePro. Essentially, it is a powerful word and word part combining and searching engine, working with databases specially designed for name creation. Let me outline a few of its many features:
• NamePro is an easy-to-learn, IBM, Microsoft Windows program.
• Databases. NamePro contains 30,000 name, and 115,000 word, databases, plus twenty-six topical databases (such as "healthcare," "sports," "value").
• Selecting, searching, combining, saving, and printing is fast and easy. Everything is automatically alphabetized too.
• The program flags preliminary trademark problems by noting the International Trademark Class number where the name has been registered and screens names for vulgarity in five languages.

As a sample naming exercise using NamePro, imagine I have to create a name for a newly-developed, lightweight garden spade.
1. From the Connotation Search window I select three databases containing words and names expressing the connotations I would like in the name: "Easy/Simple/Handy" (2199 names), "Fast/Speedy" (1911), and "Strong/Durable/Lasting" (2921). Total, 7031 names.
2. Clicking the "Combo" icon, the three are combined into a list of 6307, after eliminating duplicates.
3. I then scan the list, saving the ones I feel have potential by highlighting with the mouse and sending them to the "Keepers" list. As I scan, certain words trigger name ideas not on the list. I type them into the "Keepers" list.
4. On a quickie basis I find thirty I like, including Harmony, which strikes me as potentially part of a good family name for a line of garden tools—Harmony Gardens.
5. Unfortunately, the trademark search flags Harmony in thirty-four classes, including Class 8, Hand Tools. Harmony Gardens, however, is not flagged, because it is not in the Namebase.

   This is just a start down the name creation path for the garden spade, but it is a flying start. For further information on NamePro contact The Namestormers at (214) 350-6214.

I - 20
Project Worksheet

This worksheet is designed to help you organize your naming objectives, keep your project on course, and make it easy to keep records of successes and failures. Add questions pertinent to your situation, and skip those not applicable.

Do not write in this book. Enter the worksheet in your computer, or create a master and make photocopies. If more than one person is involved, arrive at a consensus. Of course, encourage everyone to read *Names That Sell*.

1. Begin project date:

2. Project deadline date:

3. Project chief:

4. Names of others involved (in-house and/or consulting professionals):

5. Final decision will be made by:

6. Trademark attorney:

7. Creating a new name, or reviewing an existing name?

8. Naming a company, product, service, professional office, non-profit organization, or other:

9. Lookup words, in order of priority:

10. In twenty-five words or less, what makes your company, product, or service special? How do you differ from the competition? What business are you *really* in? That done, can you reduce

it to a phrase or word?

11. Describe the ambiance or image your name should project. What *statement* do you wish to make with the name?

12. Customer profile—age, sex, income, location, sophistication:

13. Marketing range—neighborhood, city/town, county/region, national, international:

14. Frequency of use or purchase—emergency, impulse, weekly/monthly, annual, infrequent, one-time:

15. Price range, relative to competition—high, medium, low:

16. Customer benefits (most important first):

17. Emotional drives in order of importance (see Chapter II-16):

18. Names used by direct competitors:

19. Any special naming requirements you wish or require—personal names, length, sound, family:

20. List descriptive and associated words:

21. Progressive list of names created:

22. Search results; similar names in use:

23. Name-testing (marketing value) results:

24. Top three names:

25. Final choice:

26. Registration date:

27. Implementation date:

PART - II TECHNIQUES

II - 1
Your Good Name - Converting Personal Names To Business Names

Description: First (given), middle, and last names (family, surnames), initials and nicknames.

Comment: Probably the most common form of trade name.

Examples: Lydia Pinkham's vegetable compound, Wendy's Old Fashioned hamburgers, Angell & Associates.

The U.S Patent and Trademark Office considers surnames to be "descriptive" and will not register most of them as trademarks, at least not until they acquire secondary meaning. Yet personal names remain one of the most popular forms of trade names, and, to a lesser extent, trade and service marks as well.

Why? People relate to people. Even if a named person is no longer associated with the business, people like to believe they are dealing with a "real person." Thus, we have Sara Lee pastries, Mrs. Smith's pies, Marie Callender's food products, Mrs. Field's cookies—some of whom may still be active in the business, some not—and a host of similarly named enterprises in your town or neighborhood. In a personal service business or profession, such as accounting or law, people like to do business with the person whose "name is on the door." Chapter II-14 discusses naming professional firms.

When you name your business after yourself or your family, it can send a variety of messages, some subtle, some direct, some to your advantage, some not:

• The perceived distance between customer and business owner is narrowed.

• These people are proud of what they are doing. Their reputation is

on the line. They are committed, especially if they show they have
been in business for a long time.

• On the other hand, customers may associate your name too closely
with old ways and original founders. They may resist the idea of
younger members of the family taking over, moves to better locations,
changes in product lines, increases in prices, etc. These can be easier
with a less personal name. Customers may feel they can call twenty-
four hours a day to complain. Your family's privacy can be compro-
mised.

• Also, family bad apples, oddballs, or jealous relatives with the same
name can disrupt things, even if they are not directly in the business.
Family battles, estrangements, and divorces *do* happen.

I will not argue for or against using personal names. What I will do
is offer a number of techniques to help you evaluate the personal
names you are considering. Whatever you decide, I would like you
to do so after weighing all the factors you can muster. You may decide
using your personal name is not to your advantage, not good marketing strategy. Or you may decide to go ahead and use it. If you do, there
are a number of little wrinkles you can use to make your name more
distinctive—maybe not from the USPTO's (U.S. Patent and Trademark Office) perspective, but as a marketing tool.
    A problem: Many people cannot distinguish between the pride they
have in their own name, themselves, and the marketing tasks a
business name should perform. So the company gets named Hungersort
Enterprises, Inc., and that is that. Ego-trip naming? Of course it may
turn out to be Ford Motor Company, Boeing Airplane Company, or
Du Pont. Many personal names are simply not good name words. So,
before you slap all or part of your name on your CPS, ask a few
questions. We go straight back to the elements of good and great
names. Is it difficult to spell, pronounce, remember?   Is there
something unflattering about it? Is it a non-English-sounding name
people have a tough time with? Is it simply too long, too involved?
    A test: When leaving a telephone message, do you spell your name
automatically, without being asked? I do. I know a family with a
Finnish name that is really not that difficult, at least not to me. But
most people absolutely cannot deal with it. It throws them. So the

family gave up and devised a code name, like Allen, to give to dry cleaners, place on restaurant waiting lists, and leave with receptionists.

Does your name conjure up something of the negative or diminutive? Were you teased about it as a kid? Does it evoke hesitation, eye rolling, snickers, or heads turned away, even as an adult?

Does your name trigger racial, religious, or ethnic prejudice? This is, of course, a complex and emotional issue, which I do not intend to explore. I will say, however, you have a great advantage; you see it in perspective (maybe), know your goals, know your family traditions and values. And you have control, somewhat. Ask whether your name is a good marketing tool for the lengthy, broad-based task of *the business*. Try not to treat the decision as automatic, either way. That done, I am sure whatever you decide will be right for you.

Enough of the negative. Now the good part. How can you capitalize on the distinctive, in a marketing sense, aspects of all or part of your name? Failing that, how can you invent something to make it distinctive? Before I offer some positive techniques, consider:

Arnold Schwarzenegger

Early in his movie career, Arnold was advised by everyone to change his name—too long, too Austrian-sounding, impossible to spell or pronounce, simply not Hollywood. He refused. Pride? Smarts? Just stubborn? Of course, he had the right stuff, and was willing to stick it out, ending up with a marquee name.

The lesson: Arnold proved, once again, there are occasional exceptions to every rule. When we least expect it, someone is proven right for the "wrong" reasons.

Here are sixteen subtechniques for using personal names as business names:

1. Does your name have a distinctive—that word again—flair or sound, something out of the ordinary, but not too out of the ordinary? Dolby sound systems, James Cash Penney (JC Penney), Adolph Coors (Coors beer), Spreckels sugar, King Gillette (Gillette safety razors), Dr. James Crow (Old Crow whiskey), Abercrombie & Fitch sporting goods, Donald Trump real estate and casinos, Frank W.

Woolworth (Woolworth stores), Carr Chevrolet dealerships, Kitchen's Kitchens, Carson Pirie Scott department stores. William C. Durant of General Motors is said to have liked French racing car driver Louis Chevrolet's name for its musical sound.

2. Does your name have a double meaning or unusual twist, especially one that conveys the upbeat or positive. Does it flow gracefully into a logo? L.L. Bean outdoor goods and wear; Ross Dove auctioneers; Birdseye (Clarence "Bob" Birdseye, inventor of frozen food); Bell Telephone System (Alexander Graham Bell—has a nice ring to it); John Deere farm machinery (with the slogan "Nothing runs like a Deere"); Sam Goody's records, W. C. Winks hardware, Teeny Nymph (fishing fly created by Jim Teeny); Luhr Jensen (fishing lure inventor and manufacturer); Goodyear Tire and Rubber Co. (Charles Goodyear); Armstrong (various products); Cannon Mills (James William Cannon).

3. Would using both first and last name add distinction, better to catch the reader's eye? Jack Nadell Company advertising specialties, Oscar Mayer meats, Helen Bernhardt bakery, Sara Lee foods (trademark and corporate name), Johnnie Walker Scotch whiskey, Henry Weinhard's Private Reserve beer.

One of my longtime favorite corporate names was Oscar Lucks Company, a regional bakery supplier. They recently changed to the Lucks Company. One reason: The salesmen grew weary and irritated hearing receptionists announce, "The man from Oscar Mayer is here to see you." Which points up the overwhelming power of a friendly, unusual name, backed up by a commercial jingle known to every kid in America.

4. Is your name spelled in an unusual (but not too unusual) manner? Can you alter it to make it so? Browne & Co., Inc., Earle (Earle Samuels & Company), Chas. Addams (cartoonist) , Smythe, etc.

5. Does your name have instant recognition built into it? Lincoln, Jefferson, Hancock, Vanderbilt. (A friend of mine had the perfect salesman's name, Jack Dempsey. Do you think anyone forgot Jack Dempsey, the insurance salesman?) Be careful, however. Do not use

the name of a famous living, or recently deceased, person without written permission. Check with your attorney, even if your own name is identical. The more famous the person, the greater the need to do this. See Chapter II-3.

6. This goes a bit afield from using your own name, jumping into the more creative side, but maybe you can concoct a name that sounds "familiar," perhaps a bit old-fashioned, connoting that quality and goodness we long for but do not seem to find enough of these days. Orville Redenbacher's popcorn, Bartles & Jaymes wine coolers. Or, one that creates the desired image. 'Enry Beazley's fish and chip restaurant, Smokey Joe portable grill, Elmer's glue, Buster Brown shoes, Pea Soup Andersen's restaurant and motel, Mrs. Butterworth's syrup, Betty Crocker, Aunt Jemima. (Some of the above may be real people. Do you know which?)

A variation on this theme is to lend authority or friendliness with a title or modifier (even though some are totally fictitious). Papa Aldo's Take & Bake Pizza; the Dickinson Family jams and jellies; Dr. Scholl's foot-care products, 1904; Uncle Ben's Converted Brand rice; Dr. Pepper soft drink, 1885; Smith Brothers cough drops, 1852.

7. Consider using your middle name as a stand-alone, if it is a good one. One of the best theatrical titles in recent years, *Amadeus* (Wolfgang Amadeus Mozart), used this technique.

8. Use your first name only. A number of trade names and trademarks have been fashioned this way. Mercedes automobiles; Chris-Craft speedboats (builder Chris Smith); Hobie Cat catamarans (inventor Hobie Alter); Top of the Mark (Mark Hopkins Hotel); Harry and David mail-order fruit specialties; Nathan's Famous hot dogs.

9. Along with a first and last name, include a pronounceable middle initial. John F. Kennedy. Or the entire middle name. Frank Lloyd Wright, Franklin Delano Roosevelt, Hubert Horatio Humphrey, Michael Tilson Thomas, Grover Cleveland Alexander. The three-word name is not very popular today, having gone out with, say, Everett McKinley Dirkson. However, those with expansive egos who want to create a "stopper" of a name for professional, political, or theatrical reasons (and can handle it) could consider this technique.

After all, they were, or are, all marketing a product—themselves.

10. Anglicize your name for business and trade name purposes. Greenburg to Green, Szelogowski to Shelly. As discussed above, this is a very personal decision, subject to numerous considerations. The fact is, however, it has been done millions of times, and continues.

11. Abbreviate your name. Or formally adopt the abbreviation that has been tagging along all your life. Many people with jawbreaker names are known among their family and friends by shortened versions. The example above is real. For years the Szelogowski Sausage Company marketed its products as Shelly brand meats.

12. Balance your name. If you have a plain name (the proverbial Smith and Jones), add a fictitious partner (where legal and appropriate) with a highfalutin name. Smith and Charlemagne. Or, if you have a "difficult" name, pair up with Mr. Allen or Ms. Able.

13. Use individual syllables found in your name, alone or in combination. Maglite flashlight's trademark is not, as we might imagine, from the component, magnesium, as in "mag" wheels. It is from the inventor's name, Anthony Maglica. Chapter II-10 shows you how to create combination names.

14. Consider the Power "J." The initial "J" has an authoritative ring to it, a good all-purpose addition to almost any name. Use it as a leading initial (J. Edgar Hoover, J. Abigail Penobscot), or middle (Michael J. Fox). By the way, how would S. or Q. Edgar Hoover have sounded? Also, for some reason, pronounceable initials with "J" in them turn into powerful nicknames. B. J. Zeckendorf, P. J. Rachmaninoff.

15. Shake your family tree, especially the female side, for classy-sounding or euphonious names. They can be added as fictitious partners, or used alone as assumed business names (if legal and appropriate). For instance, my surname is Barrett, not great trade name potential in my opinion, although occasionally found in the business world. Throughout my family tree, I find the following: Gould (mother's maiden name), Greenfield and Chancellor (grand-

mothers' maiden names), plus Whitney, Meekins, Sharpe, Shearston, Barton, and Clausen. More potential.

16. Nicknames. After careful consideration, you might use your nickname as a trade name. Obviously, this is totally inappropriate in many cases, but sometimes it can be powerful. HoJo's from Howard Johnson's. Monkey Ward's from Montgomery Ward.

Or, invent a nickname for yourself—an opportunity you did not have as a kid, when, the more unflattering the nickname flung at you, the more likely it was to stick. Obviously, nicknames would not be used in situations where stiff formality rules. But, then again, in this age of informality, of Jimmy Carters, Joe Smiths, and Bill Clintons, who knows how formal a name should be. (I passed a government building under construction. The sign read, "William Jefferson Clinton, President of the United States." My first impression was, who the heck is that guy?) Generally, however, nicknames would be used to convey friendliness, openness, and light humor, projecting the idea that you are a nice person to do business with. An outstanding nickname business name is Kinko's Copy Centers, from the founder's nickname, given him, so the advertising literature tells us, because of the curly hair of his youth.

If you need to invent a friendly, all-purpose nickname for yourself, and possibly your company, start with Tex, Mike, Red, or Bob, and go from there. The farther out of context, the more incongruous, the more stop value, the more pay-attention value it has.

In the days of President Theodore Roosevelt, a man of nicknames himself, there was a brave and resourceful officer in the U.S. Army called Fightin' Fred Funston. From his record and deeds it could have been Fearless Fred Funston, in the flattering sense. His father did him one better. A congressman from Kansas, he had the sobriquet Foghorn Funston, and got himself elected with the slogan "Foghorn Funston, the Farmer's Friend." Do not overlook the power of alliterative nicknames; they have stick-in-the-mind quality.

II - 2
IBM You Ain't - Initials, Yuk, as Trade Names

Description: A business name made up of one or more initials taken from first letters of words, or selected at random, that are verbalized individually.

Comment: Your gift to your competitors.

Examples: CNP Woodworking, QTL Corporation, HWGA (Here We Go Again).

Names made up of initials evolve in two main ways:

1. Jerry and Joe decide to call their new company J&J Installation. Or, using their surnames, Bennett and Evans, it becomes B&E Installation. Or, if the full names were used at the start, Jerry and Joe's Installation, being somewhat of a mouthful (eight syllables), is eventually abbreviated in popular usage. The outfit may eventually adopt the shortened version as the official name. Even though these names may "work" within their spheres, I consider them mere identifiers. Although they obviously score high in spelling and pronunciation tests (Chapters I-8 and I-16), they are more difficult to remember than, perhaps, their creators imagine. They are classic examples of unimaginative names that speak to insiders, sort of, but certainly not to strangers.

2. Sometimes a respected, old-line corporation will outgrow its name, needing to modernize, to better represent its expanded scope of interests. One answer is to adopt the abbreviation it has been using all along as the official name. Sometimes this has considerable merit.
   American Machine and Foundry is a good example of the ponderous, industrial-sounding names, popular in the old days—when every catalog had an etching of a multistory, brick, smoke-spewing factory

on the cover. They pulled off a smooth upgrade to AMF Industries, retaining a dignified link with the past. Note how AMF passes the hard/soft alphabet test; no abrupt pauses.

Major corporations that have undergone similar abbreviations, officially or unofficially, include: AT&T (American Telephone and Telegraph), IBM (International Business Machines), NCR (National Cash Register), A&P stores (the Great Atlantic and Pacific Tea Company), and RCA (Radio Corporation of America. Coldwell Banker Commercial (real estate brokerage) became CB Commercial. STP additive is an abbreviation of Scientifically Treated Petroleum, certainly a mouthful. C&H Sugar is from California and Hawaiian Sugar Company—memory assisted by a nifty jingle.

Unfortunately, fashions and fads sweep through the business world just as in clothing, music, food, politics, or almost anything else. In the 1970s, or thereabouts, naming and renaming corporations with meaningless bundles of initials was one. The rationale was to create completely open-ended names, representing the outfits' intent to operate in any and every line of business—the conglomerates. J&J Installation has the advantage of at least standing for Jerry and Joe. And it is alliterative. See Chapter II-11. Folks have a chance to relate. QTL Industries stands for nothing, and people cannot relate. What QTL Industries has, that J&J does not, is a mega-budget to publicize its blunder with full-page ads in the *Wall Street Journal.*

What do you think of WYSIWYG Corporation? That is computer talk for "what you see is what you get." The example is made-up, but I did spot a company named WYNIWYG, Inc. Get it? Actually, the names are acronyms of sorts, albeit tongue twisters. Chapter II-5 discusses acronyms.

My parting shot. The big mistake people make in creating initial names, if they bother to think about it at all, is putting the cart before the horse. It is one thing for International Business Machines, with a long and distinguished history, to call itself IBM and sell its products as IBM computers. The initials *mean* something. Please do not think you can reverse the process. It seldom works. The smaller and younger you are, the less likely. Your jumble of vowelless letters fail almost all the tests, especially rememberability, which is keyed to association with something we understand. "Huh, what was that again?" They are eminently forgettable. They do not speak to strangers. They have little marketing impact.

The real shame is that there are so many truly wonderful ways to create great, or at least good, names. Why deliberately create a dud? Read on.

People respond to names that trigger recognition.

II - 3
Remember the Alamo! - Using Historic, Geographic, or Noted People's Names

Comment: Commonly used technique.

Examples: John Hancock insurance, Ethan Allen furniture, Diamond Jim's bar and grill, Patagonia sportswear, Brandywine gallery.

Is your business located in a town, city, or region with a catchy, unusual-sounding name? For example, Wausau and Oshkosh, Wisconsin; Winnebago, Iowa; and Itasca, Illinois (some of them Native American derivatives) have all become well-known business and product names.

Does your area name conjure up feelings of belonging, or them against us? Does it carry a historic or emotional charge? Carolina, Texas, Oregon, California, Brooklyn, Hollywood, San Francisco, Rocky Mountain, New York City, Alamo, Valley Forge, Concord. Does it have a famous nickname? Big Apple, Dixie, Lone Star, Hoosier, Golden Gate.

Do you want to evoke the yearning for romantic, faraway places? Do you deal in travel services, sporting goods, outdoor wear, fashion apparel, etc.? Patagonia sportswear is one of the most successful. A clever play on the names of the famous American explorers, Meriwether Lewis and William Clark, is found in Lewis N. Clark travel accessories. We recently purchased camomile tea bags from Jacksons of Piccadilly, Ltd., an actual English firm. Which has more appeal, Jackson Tea Company, for instance, or Jacksons of Piccadilly? (And what a sparkling address they list — 79 Condor Close, Three Legged Cross, Wimborne, Dorset, BH21 6SU, England.) Of course, there are the ever-popular London Fog raincoats, the name being, perhaps, more evocative, suggestive (Chapter II-9), than geographic. How many times are they selected over competitors' raincoats hanging next to them on the rack just because of the name?

The possibilities are endless. So, I have provided a number of lists to prompt your imagination in this direction—including Americana, exotic names from around the world, and beautiful names from the British Isles, found in Chapters III-5, 6, and 7.

As with surnames, geographically descriptive names are not looked upon with favor by the trademark examiners at the USPTO. Nevertheless, they remain an extremely popular naming technique, as shown in the name count list in Chapter III-28. Although not, at least immediately, registerable as trademarks, these names are registered locally as assumed business names or corporate names. Because the handful of prominent geographic names—city, state, river, compass words, mountain range—have been used so many times in every area of the country, and are somewhat generic, they must include modifiers.   Like the word *restaurant*, you cannot tie up Blue Ridge Mountains for your exclusive use.

What we have here is a big plus and a big minus. Since the names are so well known in the area, they are easy to pronounce, spell (unless it is Albuquerque), and remember. In other words, instant tradition, instant recognition. The other side is, they lack distinction, in both the trademark sense and the marketing sense. In most cases they are me-too names.

A common naming ploy is to give a broad geographic scope to impress the easily impressible, such as a neighborhood computer repair shop calling itself American Computer Systems. They are legal, I guess, but such preposterously inappropriate names irritate me. If I can, I avoid the CPSs they represent. Likewise, local outfits that use International, World, World-Wide, Global, National, and other grandiose, but inaccurate, words. Like Enterprises, these words in local business names and start-ups are sometimes tip-offs that the owner has big dreams and an expansive ego to go with them, and little else. Nothing wrong with that, I guess. But if someone advertises that they play fast and loose with the truth in one area, does it not hint they might do likewise in another? Be careful when you use these words. I must confess, however, mine is a minority view. Sad to say, these names work. For every person like me, who splits hairs and is offended, there are many who think nothing of them, trot blissfully through the door, and plunk their money down.

Noted people. I will not dwell on this technique, because I do not see new CPSs using names of presidents and the like much any more. It is somewhat old hat. (Naming streets, schools, and public buildings after people like John F. Kennedy or Martin Luther King is another issue.) However, using such a name can be considered fanciful and distinctive by the USPTO and accorded strong and immediate protection. A starter list of famous people is given in Chapter III-4.

Warning: Stay away from names of living, or recently deceased, celebrities—in sports, movies, television, politics, music—even minor-league notables and has-beens. They, or their estates, own the right to profit commercially from their fame and accomplishments, and you, in almost every instance, must pay them to share it. Get their permission in writing. Let a licensing or trademark attorney handle this for you.

Presenting a long list of examples of geographic names in use is not productive, as they are almost without number. What I will do is suggest looking beyond the five or six geographic names in your area that have been unmercifully beaten to death (again, see Chapter III-28) by conducting a search for local geographic names with a bit of panache. You might also search for not-so-famous local personages with resonant names.

"A self-made man may prefer a self-made name."
*Judge Learned Hand (after allowing Samuel Goldfish
to change his name to Samuel Goldwyn)*

II - 4
Rolling Your Own - Coined Names

Definition: To devise a new word or phrase, usually with no intrinsic meaning.

Comment: To coin a completely original trade name or trademark word is very difficult. Best leave this technique to the professionals.

Examples: Kodak, Tylenol, Corelle cookware, Scitor Corporation, Cyrix Corporation.

The breakup of John D. Rockefeller's Standard Oil Trust in 1911 resulted in a confusion of trademarks and trade names among the resulting companies. The largest, Standard Oil of New Jersey, used Esso (sort of an acronym from the initials, S.O.), Enco, and Humble (Humble Oil and Refining Company) as its trademarks.

In 1967, the corporation engaged the renowned design firm of Raymond Lowey / William Snaith, Inc., to create a new trade name and trademark. Lowey & Co. ran a computer printout of all the four- and five-letter words possible. Then, the list was progressively narrowed down to eight "strong, distinctive, and easily pronounced" words. At one of the final meetings, as the story goes, someone suggested Exxon—amazingly, a word not on the list. After exhaustive testing, the rest, as they say, is history. Too bad the originator's name isn't credited, because it was, in my opinion, a "Hall of Fame" effort. The official corporate identity changeover was made in 1972, at a cost estimated at over 100 million dollars. I remember the president of the corporation, quoted in the newspapers at the time, saying something like, "And best of all, it's all ours."

This story, even if partly hearsay, provides a good lesson for namesmiths. First, Jersey Standard and the Lowey organization did their homework, even to the extent of testing the finalist words in fifty-six languages and over one hundred dialects. (Enco failed when it was found to mean "stalled car" in Japanese.) Second, the winner was arrived at somewhat serendipitously. The question for us is, would Exxon, could Exxon, have been found without all the effort that preceded the moment of inspiration? Your answer, please.

Many years later the tanker *Exxon Valdez* ran aground, creating the disastrous Prince William Sound oil spill. The perfect name was tainted. Some said Exxon Corporation should change its name "to improve its image." Fortunately for the corporation, it was strong enough to withstand that ill-advised suggestion. To come up with a totally different, but equally successful, name, and implement it quickly, would have been almost impossible. But, in due time, they quietly rechristened the ship the *Exxon (SeaRiver) Mediterranean.*

A coined name that really works may be the ultimate—inherently distinctive, protectable from the first use, etc. That is the positive side of it. The other side: it is a difficult and high-risk naming technique. With the exception of the ubiquitous XXXCO names—which are mostly acronyms (Chapter II-5)—coining is best left to specialists. Why?

1. With all the business names in use, and all the competition for new ones—just attempting to name all of the new drugs coming onto the market each year is a staggering task—it is far more difficult to develop an original, available, and workable coined name than the novice might imagine. Computer programs have long since cast the letters of the alphabet into almost every possible combination.

Even professionals goof occasionally. Recently, a well-funded, high-tech joint venture was named Biin, which I take to be coined (unless it is an actual word or word part in a foreign language, or something like that). There were, as I recall, some European partners, which may account for what struck me as a Continental sound. The company is defunct now, so I can say I never thought much of the name, even though is was probably created by a pro, at great expense. One tip-off to a poor name is when they have to tell you how to pronounce it. In this case they did, "Byne."

2. Because a coined name, by definition, is inherently distinctive—nobody has heard of it before—and has no meaning, suggestive or otherwise, it must be force-fed to the relevant public. This can be an

expensive and time-consuming process, probably best left to wealthy corporations.

3. But the risk and expense are not necessary, because there are easier and perhaps more effective methods. Creating acronyms is one. Creating suggestive or combination names is another. Chapters II-5, 9, and 10.

But if you do it anyway and create a winner, the rewards can be spectacular. To review what has been covered earlier:

1. Coined names are inherently distinctive and warrant early and broad trademark protection.

2. Because they are unique, coined names gain value with each passing year (assuming they represent something worthwhile). Competitors have a much more difficult time inventing copycat, sound-alike names. If properly registered, used, and protected, trademarks have an indefinite life.

3. This is especially true if the coined name names a company, product, or service that is itself new. It names the idea itself, becoming what I like to call a preemptive name—the best you can get.

How do you go about coining a name?

Since I am not advocating this as a do-it-yourself technique, I will be brief. First, I would have the *Brands and Their Companies* (formerly the *Trade Names Directory*), or a directory of CPSs in your area of specialization, close at hand, so I could check my efforts quickly for duplication. Second, I would explore the various functions of an electronic dictionary—thesaurus, search, anagram. Even though they deal with actual words and word parts, they are fast, easy to use, and will provide long lists of letter combinations to get you going. Third, I would grab a thick pad of yellow paper and have at it.

II - 5
The Man from U.N.C.L.E. - Creating Acronyms

Definition: A word formed from the initial letters or parts of words.

Comment: They range from awful to some of the best.

Examples: ARCO (Atlantic Richfield Company), PIP (Postal Instant Press), CAPS (Coalition to Advance the Protection of Sports), MADD (Mothers Against Drunk Drivers).

What differentiates the acronym from the lowly string of initials that you have to say one at a time? Well-placed vowels. One of my favorite acronyms is QANTAS, the Australian airline, concocted from Queensland and Northern Territories Air Service. The fact there is no proper "qu" adds to its charm.

Here are a few pointers for creating acronyms:

• Fortunately, or unfortunately, Co., the abbreviation for Company, and Corp., for Corporation, are pronounceable. Just add it to the end of a few meaningful letters, including a vowel, and there you are. But, Co. has appeared at the end of so many acronym-type names it has little snap left. Still, every community has its hundreds of little BILCOs, ZILCOs, and MILCORPs. Some major corporations sport the technique, too, such as Sunoco and Texaco—note they have evolved into regular words without all caps—from Sun Oil Company and Texas Oil Company. Also, GEICO, Government Employees Insurance Company, and ARMCO, from American Rolling Mills. This technique produces friendly sounding, low-risk, somewhat low-impact names.

• Ideally, initials fall easily into line, forming acronyms like NATO (North Atlantic Treaty Organization). But few do. So we must get

more creative, pulling in a stray vowel or two to make them pronounceable, not just a bunch of initials. RADAR—which also is no
longer an acronym, but a regular dictionary word—was created from
RAdio Detecting And Ranging. Some near-acronyms are simply
strung-together word parts, combination names. INTERPOL, from
International Police Organization.

• Government agencies, the military, and nonprofits are great users of
acronyms. They often have so many activities to identify that they use
them for sheer survival purposes—nobody could remember all the
names without some sort of a mnemonic abbreviation. But sometimes
they, and others, go too far, resorting to forced coining, producing
what I call tortured acronyms. Some gems: ABORIGINE (Aircooled
Beryllium Oxide with Integrated Gas Turbine), MISER (Media
Insertion Scheduled Evaluation Report), and ORDEAL (Orbital Rate
Drive Electronics for Apollo and LM). Even the television show title,
"The Man from U.N.C.L.E.," has that sort of pushed-together-to-
make-it-work feeling (United Nations Committee for Law and
Enforcement).

The Navy, especially, is big on acronyms and strung-together
abbreviations. For example: NUWPNTRACENPAC (Nuclear Weap-
ons Training Center Pacific) and NAVELECSYSCOMCEN-
ATLANTDIV (Naval Electronic System Command Central Atlantic
Division).

Getting more creative, a variation on the tortured acronym idea,
creators seek catchy, appropriate words, then search around for
words, almost any words, to push into place to form an "acronym."
BOLD (Blind Outdoor Leisure Development), DARE (Drug Abuse
Resistance Education) and SOAR (Shared Outdoor Adventure Recreation) come close. Then again the acronyms are short, catchy
words. I assume they do the job. But why don't they just call them
Bold, Dare, and Soar, and forget about the forced words?

VERONICA is an Internet searching program that runs with
Gopher (a great little play-on-words name itself, from the University
of Minnesota's team nickname, the Golden Gophers). It is the
acronym of Very Easy Rodent Oriented Internet-wide Computer
Archive. Sure, it is cruel and unusual acronymishment, but since FTP
(File Transfer Protocol) has ARCHIE, Gopher *had* to have
VERONICA.

Some other well-known acronyms: ABBA, the Swedish vocal group of Agnetha Faltsbog, Bjorn Vlvaeus, Benny Anderson, and Arnie-Fred Lyngstad. Gosh, they had to do something! KISS means "Keep It Simple, Stupid," or, as recently decreed by the Vernacular Correctness Police Department (VCPD), "Keep It Safe and Simple." Radio station call letters demonstrate the power of repetition in a name when coupled with a suggestive acronym: KBCH, KCRF, KSRF, KFAN. And our friend BART, the (San Francisco) Bay Area Rapid Transit system—because they couldn't call it SFART.

• Beware of "X" in acronyms. A painful blunder I would like to forget was concocting ORXCO, Inc. (from a resurrection of the name Oregon Exchange Company, a historic 1849 outfit that produced the famous "Beaver Money" gold coins). "X" is a power letter (Chapter II-6), and very tempting, but, for heaven's sake profit from my mistake and test your X-filled acronyms. Make sure everyone pronounces them the way you do, automatically, and without prompting. In my case, much to my chagrin, everyone said, if they could say it at all, "Orks-Co." (Remember the old television show, "Mork and Mindy," with Robin Williams? "I'm Mork, from the Planet Ork.") What I was expecting was a three-syllable pronunciation, "OR-EX-CO." At the last minute, just before registering the name, I decided to change "EX" to "X," because I thought a five-letter word would look better in a logo. Snap decision, plus no testing, equalled disaster.

Here is one of my tongue-in-cheek favorites. Oregon Dental Service changed its name to ODS Health Plan, using pronounceable initials. I wonder if they realized they were also creating an acronym of sorts—Odious Health Plan? Maybe they are into oxymorons. Chapter II-20. Another, perhaps unintended, acronym was General Aniline & Film's name change to GAF Corporation.

Some interesting acronym-like names: The famous jeep of World War II fame is said to have come from the manufacturer's designation, "Government P," or an Army term, "General Purpose." Others say it was inspired by a character in the Popeye cartoon, Eugene the Jeep. Willys-Overland Motors trademarked "Jeep" in 1950, when it began producing similar vehicles for civilian sale. Talk about a name catching on! It is now a trademark of, as the ads constantly remind us, Chrysler Corporation.

Arby's restaurants came from the owners' initials, Raffle Brothers, when their first choice for a name, Big Tex, was turned down. They created a unique "A" name, always a plus, and made it friendly sounding, too. Outstanding.

Hundreds of apple varieties.
Which one has the perfect name?

II - 6
Tough Act to Follow - The Power "K" and Power "X"

Comment: The rage.

Examples: Kit Kat candy bar, Kleenex tissue, Xerox Corporation.

Some feel the super-hard "K" is the ultimate letter to include in a business name. Thus Kodak, trademark, and part of the trade name, Eastman Kodak Company. In founder George Eastman's words:

> *The letter "K" had been a favorite with me. It seemed a strong, incisive sort of letter. Therefore, the word I wanted had to start with "K." Then it became a question of trying out a great number of combinations of letters that made a word starting and ending with "K." The word "Kodak" is the result.... It became the distinctive word for our products.*

"Distinctive" is an understatement. Kodak has become the standard against which coined names are measured—perfect balance, two syllables, the Power "K," plus it passes all the other tests of a great name. Coca-Cola accomplishes much the same thing with the double "C" sound.

On the other hand, because it stands out, the "K" sound can sometimes be a laugh-getter, as in Keokuk, Iowa; Kankakee, Illinois; or Kalamazoo, Michigan. In second place is the "P" sound, which is why Podunk, with both, was the time-honored vaudeville joke locale.

Currently more popular with namesmiths is the Power "X." One of the early users was Pillsbury flour mills, as in Pillsbury's Best XXXX. XXX was an old-time baker's mark of quality, with religious significance, as in the three crosses of Calvary. The fourth "X" was added arbitrarily.

Other examples: Kotex, T. J. Maxx stores, Clorox, Syntax Corporation, Exxon Corporation, Office Max, Pyrex glass ovenware, Plax plaque loosener, Oryx Energy company (after the oryx antelope), EKCO housewares, Torx screws (from torque), Lycra Spandex, Supplex, UNIX Systems, and Galaxy everything.

P.C. Fixx illustrates a near perfect name—short, power "X," right to the point. Muzak is an old standard with a clever twist. And, of course, my old power favorite, NeXT computers.

More: Praxair, Amax, Standex Centex, Equifax, Inc., Informix Corp., Tektronix, Inc., XTRA Corp., Nextel Communication, Dylex Ltd., Ivex Holdings Corp., Methanex Corp., Ampex, Inc., Telex Communications Group, and IDEX Corp.

"The single most important marketing decision you can make is what to name the product." *Al Ries and Jack Trout*

II - 7
Toadstool Pizza Parlors - Arbitrary Names

Definition: Determined by chance, whim, or impulse. Words that have no specific meaning relative to the company, product, or service they represent.

Comment: High quality potential. Widely used.

Examples: Bicycle playing cards, Domino's pizza, Adobe software, Big Dogs clothing.

Arbitrary (or fanciful) names are divided into two distinct categories: overused (Alpha, Star, Delta, and the ilk) and underused (the rest). So, while arbitrary words form some of the most distinctive and highly protectable names in the legal sense, the more popular the word, the less effective it is, most likely, in the marketing sense.

The lists in Part III contain hundreds of arbitrary words to prime your idea pump, so they will not be repeated here. Just scan the lists, flagging, noting words that seem appropriate for your situation. Then do it again.

Please do not dismiss arbitrary names because this chapter is a short one. It is an important technique, offering endless possibilities.

Pay attention to the list in Chapter III-28, "Commonly Used Trade Names." Not to harp on testing, but be sure to check your local phone book, and eventually your state registry, to see how many other CPSs are using the same word, albeit with modifiers.

II - 8
Just Say It - Getting Right to the Point

Comment: One of the best techniques, although some names drift into the "descriptive" zone.

Examples: Brown N Serve rolls, U-Haul truck and trailer rentals, Book-Of-The Month Club, Food 4 Less.

U-Haul, as noted, has to be one of my all-time favorites—five powerful letters that are catchy, visually appealing, and contain a "buyer benefit" marketing message as well. Such a powerful marketing message, it sort of created a mini-industry. I list it in my personal Niche Name Hall of Fame, as an expression of the finest in the art of namesmithing. Please see Chapter III-27. Would it be classified as highly distinctive or merely descriptive? In my mind, it is the former.

A friend of mine, an advertising man, told of a client who invented a tool to remove spark plugs from engines, easily and without damaging the porcelain housing. Evidently it had a bright commercial future. What to call it? The friend suggested Spark Plug Puller, but the client would have none of it. He went on and on, dreaming up all manner of exotic names—inventor's license. And my friend kept saying, "Why don't you just call it the Spark Plug Puller?"

Both had their points. Spark Plug Puller leaves nothing to the imagination, but is merely descriptive, and basically unprotectable. Is this necessary, when the tool was more or less of an impulse item, sold in a display of similar tools, where there would be little doubt about what it was? Could "what it was" not be covered in a line below the name? On the other hand, the inventor's concoctions—I do not recall what they were—perhaps just attention-getters, had their place too.

A compromise, in this case, might have been to personalize the product with the inventor's first name, if it was a good one, or a fictitious name or nickname if it was not. Ozzie's Miracle Spark Plug

Puller, Howie's Original Spark Plug Puller. Not all that protectable, but they get the job done. Remember, one of the assumptions in Chapter I-7, "Our Strategy," was to get things going *now*.

Here are some more examples of Just Say It names, some using a variety of other techniques as well:

Frame & Save, 5 Minute Oil Change, HouseCheck home inspection service, Travel Pros, the Window Man, *USA Today*, Medicine Shoppe International, Browse N Barter, Delicious apples, Just for Men hair coloring.

ReaLemon juice, Ontime Delivery Company, Bag Clip snack bag closer, Office Basics, Mail-Well Envelope Co., Easy-Off oven cleaner, Real Whipped Cream, Minute Brand Original White Rice, Just Pants, Super Moist cake mix.

A Storage Place, LensCrafters, Color Back auto finish restorer, One Coater paint rollers, Quik Drip coffee maker, Factory Direct Table Pad Company, Ultra Slim-Fast diet drink, Fixall patching compound.

Power is a power word.

II - 9
Just Imply It - Suggestive Names

Definitions: Imply: To express or indicate indirectly. Suggest: To call to mind by logic or association; evoke.

Comment: Excellent technique for the do-it-yourself namesmith.

Examples: Pepperidge Farm bakery products, Rainy Day bookstore, Campfire marshmallows, Snapple beverages, Spam luncheon meat.

Following on the heels of "Just Say It" we have the potent and logical technique; just suggest it, just imply it, just evoke it.

Because these names are less obvious and direct, they are considered inherently distinctive and given broad protection. Some examples given are probably not technically suggestive, in the USPTO sense, but that is not our main concern. This is a marketing book. Classification is made more confusing because many names are an amalgam of suggestion and other techniques, such as combinations of words or word parts. Chapter II-10.

Perhaps the best way to give you a how-to heave-ho is by throwing a long line of examples:

Glade air freshener, Winn-Dixie stores, Sleighbells Christmas Shops, Meow Mix cat food, Grandma's Table restaurant, Slice beverage, Safeway Stores, Inc., Snow Crop frozen foods, Kool-Aid (1927), Treesweet apple juice, Miller High Life beer, Eskimo Pie frozen confection, Sani-Flush toilet bowl cleaner.

Sunkist oranges, Sun-Maid raisins, *Playboy* magazine, Holiday Inn motels, Orange Crush beverage (1916), Mennen products for men,

Pocket Books, Cat's Paw shoe soles and heels, Coppertone suntan lotion, Cream of Wheat cereal (1893), You're Hired job search software, Pierce-Arrow automobiles, Hot Lips pizza, Talon zippers, A Taste Devine catering service, Swiss Miss hot chocolate mix.

Ray•Ban sunglasses, Vise-Grip locking pliers, First Alert smoke alarms, Sizzler Family Steak House, IncoTax tax service, Spring Green lawn care, Manpower, Inc., temporary services, Pedigree Pet Centers, Ten Forty tax service, Putt Putt golf courses, the Men's Wearhouse, Roughneck spitting wedge, Diagnostek, Inc., Sanifill, Inc.

Big League Chew (bubble gum shredded to look like chewing tobacco), Presto cookware, Fun Gun food decorator, Eggcrate brand products, Krypton flashlights, Charger rechargeable flashlight, Instapure water purifiers, Elmer's glue (Elsie the Borden cow's husband — "tough as a bull, but friendly too."), Tide and Rinso detergents, Jell-O dessert, Resolution Trust Company, Resumé (Talbots women's "career wardrobe.").

Levolor blinds, Able Body Company dump truck bodies, Village Blacksmith tools, Credo drill bits, Turtle Wax automobile finish, Hot Wheels toy cars, GrandMa's cookies, Baker's chocolate, "Hello" telephone products catalog, Pampers and Huggies disposable diapers, Hi-C beverages, Progresso foods, Tang breakfast drink, Ritz crackers.

Nature Valley granola, Acutrim for weight loss, Velveeta cheese spread, J. Crew preppy clothing catalog, Foot Locker sports apparel, the Sharper Image state-of-the-art-electronics, Cyclone fence, Whirlpool washing machines, Little Black Book address software program, Candy Barrel candy stores, All Week Long (Eddie Bauer's professional women's clothing store), Cap'n Crunch cereal, Crawdaddy's Creole Cooking restaurant.

Suggesting authority

An effective variation is to incorporate an authority figure, or title, into your name. This technique is currently quite popular. One word of choice is *choice*. President's Choice specialty foods, Critic's Choice videos, Taster's Choice coffee. Mr. Coffee and Mr. Goodwrench do somewhat the same thing, as do Burger King and Captain Ahab's restaurants, the Baron of Belmont cafe, Monarch Financial Group, and the Glass Doctor ("We fix your panes.").

Another authority ploy is positioning your CPS ahead of your competition with the power word *The*. I like this technique and hope you explore it if it holds any potential in your situation. The Masters golf tournament, The Ohio State University, The Place restaurant. One of my favorite slogans is "*The* Resort on the Oregon Coast," used by Salishan Lodge.

Creating preemptive names

Preemptive: Having the power to preempt or take precedence.

Build a word like *best*, *first* or *perfect* into your name, words that foreclose the idea in the customer's mind that anything could possibly be better, or could come before. WordPerfect may, or may not, be the best word-processing program on the market, but it has a preemptive name, suggesting—asserting?—that it produces perfect words, perfect business letters, perfect manuscripts, and is, in fact, *the* perfect program. I like Lotus 123 for the same reasons. If the spreadsheet problem was "hard to learn and hard to use," and Lotus solved it, what better name than one suggesting it is "easy as one, two, three"? Can a rival top that name?

Some other power words and names: Paramount Pictures, Baker's Secret, Apex, Progressive, Integrity, Prime, Ultra, Master, Prestige, Eclipse, Magic, Giant, Original Gardenburger, Impact Publishers, Strong Opportunity fund, All detergent, Big Mac (McDonald's) and the Whopper (Burger King) hamburgers, Manpower, Inc., temporary services. For more ideas, see the list in Chapter III-9, "Superlatives - Laudatory, Power, and Action Words."

PowerMaster, a combination of two power words, was proposed to name a high-alcohol-content malt liquor, targeting inner-city blacks. But the U.S. Bureau of Alcohol, Tobacco, and Firearms would not allow it because they thought the name was *too* effective. Which leads us to:

Targeting your customer

Most of the naming techniques in this book involve targeting in one way or another—that is the idea. Without trying to delve into political correctness, I would like to bring up a few names targeting racial, religious, or ethnic groups, or used in reference thereto, in a defamatory, or perceived defamatory, way. Of course, giving a restaurant an ethnic or suggestive name, indicating the type of cuisine served, is not what I am talking about.

For over sixty years, Colgate-Palmolive Company sold a toothpaste in Asia called Darkie. The logo was a caricature of a minstrel in blackface, reputedly inspired by Al Jolson. Asians, it seems, took no offense, but American interest groups forced a change. Now it is Darlie toothpaste, with a neutral, but similar-looking, character in the logo.

On a more subtle note, we find a brewery creating Crazy Horse malt liquor, and cigarette companies targeting ethnic groups with Uptown and Dakota brand cigarettes. After protests and government pressure, the names were scrapped.

Even college and professional sports team names and nicknames referring to American Indians can offend. The irony is that some were adopted to honor, not to defame. Most of the colleges have changed, however, including Dartmouth, Stanford, St. Johns, etc. Only a few professional teams hold out: the Cleveland Indians, Atlanta Braves, Kansas City Chiefs and, most notably, the Washington Redskins football team.

What is left? Scottish names and words playing to their supposed thriftiness and frugality, the Dutch to cleanliness, Irish to drinking, etc., still exist. Scotch brand tape, Plaid Pantry convenience stores, McTweedy motel, Dutch Girl cleanser, Thistle Inn, Delaney's pub, Holland restaurants, Dutch Boy paints, Quaker Oats, Windmill bakery.

Offensiveness aside, I believe ethnic targeting and suggestiveness have lost their effectiveness, descending into the category of crude, unsophisticated naming. Passé, they belong to an age best forgotten, having no more place in modern naming and marketing than Little Black Sambo's restaurants.

If you wish to appeal to the price-conscious buyer with your name, use better words. Thrifty motel, Budget car rental, Economy gas station, Dollar car rental. Of course, use them honestly. On a recent trip, my wife and I found a "Budget" motel that, after looking around, turned out to be the highest priced in town.

Altering suggestive words to make them unique

A great example is Compaq Computers. The word *compact* was thought to have a favorable, dominating theme. It was changed by substituting *q* for *ct*. The theme was retained, somewhat, and a distinctive new trademark and trade name was created. Brilliant, really.

Please note, Compaq was not created over lunch, on the back of an envelope. It was professionally done, the product of extensive effort and research. After the fact it seems easy, just switch a few letters. Before the fact, something else again.

Is this a technique for do-it-yourself namesmiths? Not for the most part. But it is possible. And, as I mentioned in Chapter II-4, "Coined Names," if you do create a winner, you might create a huge winner. Do not be dissuaded. Just be aware: this, for the most part, is a high-risk technique. Also, do not confuse this technique with altering words by the use of stylized spelling, covered, somewhat, in Chapter II-22.

Some other thoughts: Take the adjective *accurate*, "conforming exactly to fact, errorless." Drop one of the *c*'s and the *te* on the end, and you have the Acura automobile. Sentra is probably from *sentry*, suggesting security and dependability. Lumina would seem to be created the same way, and perhaps it was, but it is in the dictionary, the plural of lumen, which is a measure of light.

Add an *a* to the word *garden*, and you get Gardena, a beautiful-sounding trademark for garden products. Who knows exactly how Muzak was created; just playing around with *music*? Changing *crayon* to Crayola created a trademark suggesting activity. Torx drive screws are from *torque*. Eggo frozen waffles. Take away half of luxury and you have Lux soap.

One of the best word alterations, or abbreviations, from my point of view, is Nilla wafers, by Nabisco. The product, vanilla cookies, is aimed at kids. The name is pure kidspeak. Another friendly, suggestive name with a long, happy life is Wheaties. Intel Corporation comes from, presumably, the word *intelligent*, the word part being far more powerful as a name than the whole. I also like Humana, Inc., the hospital chain. Try to top that one.

"The Ancient Mariner would not have taken so well if it had been called *The Old Sailor." Samuel Butler*

II - 10
Please Don't Eat the Morphemes - Combination Names

Definition: Names made up of one or more words and/or word parts, with partial or complete meaning retained.

Comment: One of the best do-it-yourself naming techniques.

Examples: CompuServe, Omnicom, Branola, Teleflora, Comsat, Envirosource, Trinova, Qualcomm, Inc.

This technique is one reason I suggest you stay away from pure coined names. It is far easier to use, and the names created, if they make any sense at all, have little chance of bombing.

It is not a technique, however, completely without risk, as one can see from the number of corny, ill-conceived names floating around out there. On the other hand, many creators knew full well the names were corny. That is exactly what they wanted.

As with so many of the techniques in Part II, there is no single magic formula, as there are so many possibilities. So, I will again shower you with examples. Hopefully, after seeing enough, and plugging them into your own situation, you will say, "Hey, I can do that." Some combinations are obvious and straightforward, even though naming big-time companies, products, and services—just press two words or word parts together. Ford Windstar minivan. Others are pretty darned clever.

Adidas is from the shoe company founder's name, Adi Dassler. Unisys (Unified Systems). ConAgra (Consolidated Agricultural). A few years back, the *Trade Names Directory* listed seventy-two pharmaceutical products beginning with *geri*, from *geriatric*. The best known, of course, is Geritol. Victorinox is one of the official Swiss Army knife makers. It is a combination of the founder's mother's name, Victoria, and an early name for stainless steel.

One of the most successful combination names is Jazzercise, which passes the pronunciation tests with flying colors. Noxzema is a combination derived from a stylized spelling of *knocks* and one of the ailments it supposedly cured, eczema. It is close to being a coined word. Sanka brand beverage is from *sans* and *caffeine*, though, like Noxzema, probably few customers pick up on the derivation.

Vaseline, the name, was created in 1859, supposedly from *water* in German and *olive oil* in Greek. Pepto-Bismol is partly from the word *eupepsia* or *eupeptic*, relating to good digestion. (Greek eu = well, and peptin = to digest.) Murine (eye drops) is from its ingredients, muriate and berberine. Cutex, from *cuticle* and *ex*. Coca-Cola comes from two of its original ingredients: South American coca leaves and African cola nuts. Formica laminated plastic was originally developed as a substitute for mica, used as an electrical insulator. Thus the name, for mica.

Some more recent, or not-so-recent, combinations: WearEver aluminum ware; Toastmaster; Mixmaster; Rubbermaid; Twistup cork puller; DriZair moisture remover; Lumilite flashlights; Instapure water purifiers; Powerlock flexible tape measures; Delimex Mexican delicatessen; Gatorade, from the nickname of the University of Florida football team; Bisquick; Texsun grapefruit juice.

Threepeat, a clever new word, meaning to win three titles in a row, was trademarked by coach Pat Reilly. Or so we are told ad nauseam on the sports radio talk shows. *Megatrends*, the book title, was trademarked by author John Naisbitt. And Florafax, Procardia heart medicine, Glucotrol for diabetics, Venturcom, Microsoft, LaserJet, Primerica, and NutraSweet. Citibank is from First National City Bank of New York.

Amtrak is a very smooth name, one of the best. It was created by Lippincott and Margulies, the famous corporate image and design firm, to replace Railpax, which "sounded like a box lunch," Hallowed in the computer world is VisiCalc, the original spreadsheet program, the visible calculator.

How to:

To begin, simply start a list from your head, the dictionary, brainstorming, etc. Be sure to consider emotionally suggestive words as discussed in Chapter II-16. Next, isolate the word parts that strike you as the most powerful, meaningful. Compu from computer. Serve from service. Then mix, match, combine, and run all the basic tests.

Try to limit your combination name to two or three syllables. Hyphenating words or word parts is mostly passé for names today.

Very popular—one could almost call it a fad—is the practice of capitalizing the first letter of the second word or part. OreIda potato products, ChemLawn. I like this technique. It is reader friendly, flagging the name, making it stand out, stating, in effect, this word was created specifically to name something. Overdone or not, give this one a look.

Doubling up. If the last letter or two of the first part and the first letter or two of the second part are the same, so much the better. CycLearning (listening to foreign-language tapes while riding an exercise bicycle), Goldome Bank, Electricord, ReaLemon, Accountemps (accounting temporaries), TraveLodge. Harvestore silos pull a double.

Pay careful attention, however, to the pronunciation, and hard/soft letter tests. Some of the above, in my opinion, pass, and some are borderline. Another test, of course, is whether you have to explain it. And your private test. Sit on the name for a time. It may not seem so terribly clever next week.

Then, there is the ever-popular variation of abbreviating a word and tacking on Co. or Corp. This creates an acronym-like name, which, while not terribly imaginative, as mentioned in Chapter II-5, has its place.

"Fate tried to conceal him by naming him Smith."
Oliver Wendell Holmes, Jr.

II - 11
The Prattle Factor - Alliteration and Rhyme

Alliteration

Definition: An alliterative name consists of two or more words with similar initial sounds.

Comment: Big medicine.

Examples: Roto Rooter drain-cleaning service, Lint Lifter clothing cleaner, Super Soaker squirt guns, Intel Inside.

Tell me, how many bouncing baby boys have you seen lately? Are all girls good girls? Are all boys bad boys?

That is alliteration, folks. The words roll off the tongue so smoothly, the fine points of meaning can easily get lost in the repetition. Mindless repetition sometimes. I call it the prattle factor.

The idea in creating alliterative business names is to get the prattle factor going in your favor. Make no mistake about it, people love to repeat alliterative names. And the more they repeat them, the better they are remembered, and repeated by others.

Plus, these musical names have a bonus: the field is relatively uncrowded. Another bonus: unlike many coined names or acronyms, alliterative names usually do not sound contrived. It is a wonderful technique for the do-it-yourselfer.

And yet another: Unlike its cousin, rhyme, alliteration does not even have to be done correctly. Almost any series of words with the same initial letter or sound—Kona Coffee—will generate an alliterative effect, often as good as if the sound was created "properly," using two or more letters. Master Mend, Planters Peanuts, Midas Mufflers. Remember, we are not talking grammatical precision, we are talking marketing. It is the effect upon the casual, often disinterested receiver that counts.

Of course, anything can be pushed to ridiculous extremes. Take Carter's Little Liver Pills, concocted in 1870. Two of its bald-faced imitators were Dr. William's Pink Pills for Pale People and Dr. Wilson's Blue Pills for Blue People. Another bomb was Kandy Kake candy bars. Rechristened Baby Ruth, they have been doing nicely ever since.

Even staid professional firms can benefit from arranging names to form an alliteration. Previously mentioned Alex Osborn's advertising firm was called Batton, Barton, Durstine and Osborn. When two firm member's names are the same, you get the benefits of alliteration without even trying. Rosen, Rosen and Stemple. Then, of course, simply repeating any name gives the effect. Putt Putt miniature golf courses, Circus Circus casinos.

Other alliterative and alliterative-like business names: Home Helpers, Corner Caddy, Tuck tapes, Tony Roma's Baby Back Ribs, Brooks Brothers clothiers, Hobby Horse antiques, Plush Pippin pie shops, Minute Maid orange juice, Calico Corners fabric stores, Better Business Bureau, Dunkin' Donuts, Fanny Farmer Candies, Dave's Deli.

California Cooler, Bob's Big Boy restaurants, Farmer's Friend hand salve, Northern Nectar maple syrup, Red Rose tea, Cascade Kids clothing, Libby, McNeill & Libby, Red Robin restaurants, Earthquake Ethyl's road house, Premier Press, Pumpkin Patch U-pick farm, and, if you are old enough to remember, Tinkertoys.

Do-it-yourself hint: Remember the electronic dictionary.

Rhyme

Definition: Rhyming names are composed of two or more words with corresponding terminal sounds.

Comment: Of limited use in business naming.

Examples: Shake 'n Bake, Nite Lite, Stable Table.

My enthusiastic recommendation of the alliteration technique does not carry over to rhyme Rhyming names are tricky, the reason being they come across as friendly, lighthearted, even laughter provoking. This may be just what you want, as in Lucky Ducky Day Care Center or Fuzzy Wuzzy Rug Company. But if you have a more formal CPS, watch out, the prattle factor can work against you if the name can be repeated in a derisive-sounding or singsong manner. And that is what rhyming is, somewhat singsong.

Some more rhyming names: Scrubby Buddy sink cleaner, Slack Rack, Quik Pick lint brush, Night Sight flashlight, Lean Cuisine frozen meals, Gentle Dental, Famous Amos cookies, Ragin' Cajun cafe, Dick Blick Company, Sony Only, Osh-Kosh children's clothing, Double Bubble gum, Full Sail ale, Rent A Dent rental cars, Dr. Pepper soft drink, Fill Yer Belly Deli, Tower of Power ultrasonic cleaner, Piggly Wiggly stores, Mars bars, Tutti-Frutti gum.

What a difference
a letter or two makes.

ape - axe
bra - brie
free - fry
tide - bride
lie - lye
gun - bun
hell - hello
elm - elf
can - cane
kill - kiln
fox - fax

II - 12
Secret Weapon - Onomatopoeia

Definition: Onomatopoeic words imitate the sounds associated with the objects or actions they represent. Put differently, the words themselves sound like what they describe.

Comment: Big dividends if handled well.

Examples: Sizzler Steak House, Talon Zipper.

DZZZT, DZZZT, DZZZT, DZZZT, DZZZT, DZZZT, CLICK. (From a U.S. West Communications advertisement.) Although possibly a little far-fetched, these words are onomatopoeic attempts at representing a telephone busy signal, then hanging up in frustration.

Let us try another example, a name that may not seem onomatopoeic to you, but does to me: J. M. Smucker's jams and jellies. The name conveys the idea that its products are "lip-smacking good." And, because it sounds old-fashioned, it gives the impression the company has been in business a long time. (If it had not *really* been around for a long time you would think it had been dreamed up by a calculating namesmith.) Not only that, but the company lives in a place with a pretty nifty-sounding name to match, Orrville, Ohio. I have no idea where it is, but from the sound of it, it cannot be very big. What mental image do you get from the whole package; Grandma stirring up a batch of jam on the wood stove, or the day shift at the factory cranking out another zillion gallons?

I like Fiskars, the cutlery company. It fits right in with the word *scissors*, the sound of shearing something, all seeming to have onomatopoeic overtones.

How about Talon Zipper Company. Talon (claw) is a good suggestive name, and zipper is as good an onomatopoeic word as you can get. The word *zipper* has an interesting story. Over the years, as the device itself was being perfected, the name was too. Some early attempts were "clasp locker" and "Plako." In hindsight, they were clearly struggling. An early manufacturer called itself the Hookless Fastener Company. Not bad, describing the gadget's first use, replacing irritating, time-consuming high-top shoe hooks. "Zipper" was reputedly coined in 1921 by an employee of the B.F. Goodrich Company, when the president called for an "action word" that would "dramatize the way the thing zips."

An old joke defines an intellectual as someone who can listen to the *William Tell* overture and not think of the Lone Ranger. Can you say the name Roto Rooter and not think of the jingle?

> *Roto Rooter, that's the name.*
> *And away go troubles down the drain.*

Is there a business name, slogan, and jingle combination as successful and enduring? It has alliteration—Ro, Ro. The *o*'s have a rhythmic effect. The words are suggestive and onomatopoeic (at least they seem so to me)—Rrrrrrrrroto Rooooooooter. Can't you hear those Ro-Tos and Roo-Ters rrrrripping into all that bad stuff blocking your drain? *O* is a good soft letter, and *R* is a nice HARD one. Both words have two syllables, thus good cadence. Over the years it has certainly benefited from the prattle factor.

Roto Rooter's catchy, almost impossible to forget jingle reinforces the name. In fact, that is exactly what it says, "that's the name." Top that off with a strong emotional appeal — troubles gone, out of sight, out of mind, and with no effort by you. Plus, an unbeatable close with the idiom, "down the drain," and you have, perhaps, the ultimate. No wonder Roto Rooter is the most imitated name in the Yellow Pages — Ready Rooter, Redi Rooter, Rescue Rooter, Mr. Rooter, Rooter Man, Super Rooter, and many more.

A short onomatopoeic word list: Buzz, chop, click, clink, dribble, fizz, glop, grunt, gurgle, hiss, plop, rip, snap, splash, swish, thud, thump, tinkle, whir, whoosh, woof.

Express your creativity: Scrunch Bros. auto wrecking, Gurgle & Trickle Plumbing Co., Slither and Hiss snake farm.

II - 13
The Belch Fire 8 - Numeric and Alphanumeric Names

Definition: "Consisting of or utilizing letters, numbers ... and other conventional symbols."

Comment: Especially popular for products and product lines.

Examples: 7UP soft drinks, Formula 409 cleanser, MX-5 Miata model Mazda automobile, 3Com Corp.

You have been working on your invention for five or ten years. You are forming a company to produce and sell it. Your patent is pending. The financing is in place. Over those long years you have produced eighteen painfully crafted prototypes of your gizmo-whatchamacallit-gadget, each one slightly better than the one before. Now you have the little beauty in your hand, along with a stack of bills, and a very expensive injection mold. Last, in most cases, but not least, you need a name. "Hey, that's what we'll call it, Product 18!"

Eighteen is a number loaded with emotion and meaning for you and your development partners. It is not, however, loaded with emotion and meaning for your potential customers. All Mr. and Ms. Stranger/Customer care about is, "What will the darn thing do for me? Where can I get it? How much does it cost?" Your new company and/or product name's job is to get their attention, tell them what it is about, and pique their interest—not to immortalize your struggle.

But many famous companies and products have names with numbers in them, you say. Phillips 66 gasoline, Baskin-Robbins 31 ice cream stores, A-1 steak sauce (and one hundred other A-1 products), WD-40 all-purpose lubricant, 7-Eleven convenience stores, 3M Company.

The Belch Fire 8, by the way, is from "Grin and Bear It" in the Sunday funnies. For years it has been the cartoonist's stock automobile name for his many jokes cast in automobile dealers' showrooms. A recent cartoon takes a different slant. The picture shows a long line of cars entering a national park. A park ranger in a booth announces through his megaphone, "Only cars with animal names beyond this point!"

Back to our business. Remember, however, 3M Company is an alphanumeric abbreviation of an old and respected company name, Minnesota Mining and Manufacturing Company, nicely alliterative, but too long. Like IBM, it did not start out with the shortened version.

Another with a clever twist is CH^{2}M, an abbreviation of Cornell, Howland, Hayes and Merrifield, the giant engineering firm. Today they are CH^{2}M-Hill. I wonder why they did not make it CH^{3}M. Maybe it was too close to.... Never mind.

Most of the examples above are firmly entrenched in the public consciousness, and are therefore good names. Although I will not attempt to dissuade you as I did in Chapter II-2, "Initials," numeric and alphanumeric names are definitely in the "create and handle with care" category. Think long and hard before you attempt to push an unusual number, such as 73, 155, or even 18 on the public. The reason: People need something to "grab hold of," something to relate to. Belch Fire 8 is at least suggestive. Product 18 suggests nothing.

A few more observations:

First or 1st has long been a favorite, especially for financial institutions. A power word, it is defined as "before or above all others in time, order, rank, or importance," the very essence of a preemptive name. But "first" can be loosely defined to apply to almost anything, so the meaning is watered down. Do you know if the First National Bank in your town really was the first bank in town?

Two or 2nd is all right if it does not carry the feeling of second best or second place. That is a turnoff for most Americans. On the other hand; if the meaning is "double", or "twice as good", that is fine. I like the Mexican beer name XX Dos Equis. Or, as the dudes around here say, Dos Ekkies.

Three and seven are magic numbers—Tri, Three, 3, Triple, 7, Seven. Four and five are not too commonly used, except when the implication is of four or five stars, popular in rating movies, hotels, motels, and restaurants.

Stick with the simple (1 - 13) and alliterative (33, 66) numbers, and a few others (76, 100, 101). They have the advantages of being easy to pronounce and understood by all. Some may contain meaning, such the operating hours of 7-Eleven stores. Others may be obliquely suggestive. Do you really get a room for six bucks at Motel 6 or eight bucks at Super 8 Motels? And, of course, many numbers come with ready-made memory aids: sayings and tag lines. Three yards and a cloud of dust. Seven come eleven. Eight ball. Cheaper by the dozen. Perfect 10. Batting a thousand. Baker's dozen. Nine lives. Spirit of '76. Route 66.

One of the oldest number names is 3-In-1 compound, 1895, the first branded lubricant. 7UP is close to a perfect name, with the lucky seven number and the upbeat word *up*. Another would be Seagram's Seven Crown whiskey. Four Roses whiskey. Jack Daniel's Old Time (Old No. 7) Quality Tennessee Sour Mash Whiskey, dating back to 1857.

Intel Corporation had great success with the "86" series of computer chips, 8086, 286, 386, and 486. But the numbers could not be trademarked, and imitators used them. So, when they launched the next generation, the "586," they called it the Pentium (Greek < *pente*, five).

Add complete address,
including communication numbers,
each time a name is printed.

I - 14
Pierce, Fenner and Beane - Naming Professional Offices

Profession: An occupation requiring considerable study and specialized training.

Comment: There are many more naming options available today than in the past.

Examples: Kenge and Carboy, Living Trust Law Offices, the Rose Law Firm.

We no longer live in communities of continuity, where generation after generation live out their lives, where everyone knows everyone else. Simply hanging out one's shingle can be the slow road (or dead end) to establishing a successful practice.

These are the days of marketing professional services. Advertisements proliferate in the Yellow Pages, in other print media, and on radio and television, unheard of ten years ago, along with a new breed of nontraditional, attention-grabbing professional office names. Willie Johnson's Bankruptcy Express, Gentle Dental.

However, depending upon the profession, there are state laws and codes of ethical conduct established by the associations that still must be adhered to. For instance, names leading customers to believe a firm is larger than one person are usually prohibited, if there is only one person involved. False advertising. Some states prohibit using names of partners not currently active in the firm. Others do not, allowing the evolution of ongoing, fixed, or corporate professional names, such as Arthur Andersen, the huge accounting firm. Some have a time limit for phasing out the name of a retired or deceased partner or owner. Some allow practice under an assumed business name other than one including some or all of the partners.

Since you must follow the *latest* regulations in your state or area,

it is pointless to attempt to summarize them here. Look them up.
Depending upon the leeway your have, your specific profession, and,
especially, the personalities involved, you might consider:

• Reviewing Chapter II-1, "Personal Names." The techniques given
are just as applicable in the professions as regular businesses.
Marketing quality is marketing quality.

• Did the firm operate with the same name for many years? Is it
established in the relevant public's consciousness? Were some of the
partner's names so unique they just "worked," clicked with everyone.
Was the firm name so arranged, for whatever the reason, to contain
the perfect number of words and syllables, to flow nicely, easily,
memorably? Was someone famous—senator, judge, governor—way
back? Do the names of the new partners replacing the old-timers
"have it"? Must the senior partner's name be at the beginning or end
of the string, even if it sounds terrible? Must every partner be listed
at all, the "name on the door" syndrome? If permissible, would it be
to your marketing advantage to adopt a "once-and-for-all" name?
    I've always liked the name of the New York law firm of Cravath,
Swain and Moore, known simply, I have heard, as Cravath, or the
Cravath firm. It *sounds* like a law firm to me. I imagine it is a fixed
name now, but do not know. As for a firm with a truly distinctive
string of names, try this one: Skadden, Arps, Slate, Meagher & Flom.
Another good one: Touche, Ross, Bailey, Niven, and Smart (or
something like that), which has been merged and changed so many
times I do not know what remains. Haskins & Sells is, or was, a perfect
accounting firm name. Can't you visualize a corps of diligent
accountants, sitting on high stools with their green eyeshades, hunched
over leather-bound ledgers? Or today, steely-eyed CPA/MBAs,
rattling their computer keyboards, their screens blurred with numbers. It would be going too far to suggest the longevity of some of the
great professional firms had much to do with their names. But, then
again, over the years, somebody had to make the choice of whom to
call—thousands and thousands of times.
    Another one of my favorite old-time names was the investment firm
of Glore, Forgan, Wm. R. Statts Company. What a delightfully
appropriate-sounding name. Was it was merged out of existance as

Du Pont Glore Forgan or did it die in one of Wall Street's frequent blood-lettings?

• Of course the "working name" of the firm usually becomes the first one or two words. Touche Ross. Plan for this. Anticipate the nickname. Be certain it is favorable. Do not allow the competition to concoct something unflattering, because, if it is at all possible, they will. We all know Merrill Lynch, which used to have the wonderful handle, Merrill Lynch, Pierce, Fenner and Beane. "Beane" had that catchy terminal sound, like the boom of a base drum in the band. Then Mr. Beane was replaced by a Mr. Smith. What a letdown for the names connoisseur.

• The partners' names can be arranged so the initials are easy to say. Again, since the formal name came first, and is more or less obligatory, initials are okay. The architectural firm of Skidmore, Owings and Merrill has a mellow sound. Its pronounceable initial nickname, S-O-M, also works well. It has a pleasant, consonant-vowel-consonant, hard-SOFT-soft, makeup, but is not quite an acronym.

• Acronyms for professional firms. Be very careful. Keep cleverness under control. I know of more acronyms for professional firms that do not work than do. JAMS - Judicial Arbitration & Mediation Services. Test thoroughly for the "laughing with you, or laughing at you?" factor. Aside from the ridiculous-sounding ones, the problem is marketing. The insiders and those who deal with the firm every day will pick up on just about anything. But a vague acronym may cause strangers to draw a blank. "What the heck is this? What are they talking about?" In some cases it may be well to arrange the names so they deliberately do *not* form an acronym.

• Can the firm operate with a formal name *and* a marketing name? Although traditionalists consider this undignified and unprofessional, in the competitive marketplace it is becoming increasingly popular. The most-used strategies stress location or specialty. So, we have the Broadway Clinic, Southwest Tax Preparation, or Gentle Dental. Gentle Dental is a terrific name—short and to the point, understandable, memorable because it rhymes, and friendly, through a well thought out play on the emotions.

• Here is a pattern for an ideal professional firm name. Of course, you have to have the right-sounding names to begin with. But we do the best we can. For our exercise, we will concoct the law firm of Templeton, Asquith and Strong.

The name has ideal cadence and sends a professional message. Templeton is a name that commands respect. Dignified. It forces the reader or speaker to slow down. There are no pronunciation problems, however, even though it is a three-syllable word.

Asquith is one of those quirky, offbeat-type names that give sparkle to certain professional firm names. They are to be treasured. (Sometimes, however, the names sound so off-the-wall, one wonders if they represent real people, now or ever. This example, of course, comes from Herbert Henry Asquith, British prime minister from 1908 to 1916.) The unusualness of the name offsets possible pronunciation problems. Two syllables.

Strong is a power terminal word, bringing the reader or speaker up short. Finality. Authority. One syllable. Just what we want.

So, we have a three-two-one syllable cadence, which rolls nicely off the tongue. It sends a message to the client that he is dealing with a professional firm of substance and tradition, just what most clients *want* to deal with. And, we have no "hard" ending letter followed by a "hard" beginning letter, which, for the most part, is to be avoided; although, as stated earlier, it is sometimes desired.

The shortened versions of the name might be Templeton Asquith, the Templeton firm, the Asquith firm, or the Strong firm, all acceptable. Since *A* is a vowel, the initials form something of an acronym, TAS, but it is unlikely to be a problem, since the full name, or any of the shortened versions, are so easy to say.

In short, the keys to using this professional naming formula are: Use unique names to maximum marketing advantage. Save the shortest, one-syllable if possible, strongest-sounding name for last. Stay close to the three-two-one syllable makeup. Next best: three-one-two.

II - 15
Hug Your Tree - Naming Nonprofit Organizations

Definition: Not seeking or producing a profit or profits.

Comment: Number one problem—verbosity.

Examples (good): Make-A-Wish Foundation, Save the Children, March of Dimes.

Nonprofit organizations often have to cram some very important words into their names—Association, International, Federation, Fellowship, Organization, Foundation, Conference, Independent, Community, Institute. But gee! The International Association and Hall of Fame of (insert whatever it is about)? One might as well go all the way, and add a touch of tongue-in-cheek humor, as in the Society for the Preservation and Encouragement of Barbershop Quartet Singing in America—SPEBQSA.

A few tips:

Remember, many computer database setups only have room for a limited number of letters and spaces. I have seen nonprofit names chopped off before they got to the words at the end telling what the organization did, what it was all about.

Ask yourself, does the name really need all those jawbreaker, multisyllable words? Or are they in there simply to sound like a nonprofit "ought to sound." Nonprofits have to speak to strangers too—like during fund raising-time (which is all the time). You may find it beneficial to review the name length and syllable count suggestions in Chapter I-16, "Testing Your Name."

Does the name contain words not found in the average person's vocabulary? Can simpler words be found? One wonders whether some nonprofit name words are deliberately selected to confound.

Many organizations use a standard formula: Location (city, state, region, national), plus designator (Association, etc.), plus "of," plus (whatever it is about). The question is, what is most important? What word should come first? Some organizations have their reasons (local chapter, tradition) for sticking to the formula, but, if you have a clean slate, you might consider leading with your lookup word. See Chapter I-14.

Some trade associations, tight little groups which do not have to do much marketing or fund raising, may simply not care about the fine points of naming. To others, letting the public know it is of national scope is very important, justifying lead words like *American* or *National*. The word *International*, in my opinion, should not be used unless it is truthful, conveying genuine meaning, not just a wished-for state of affairs. Also, it can be a red-flag word, arousing skepticism in sophisticated readers, because it appears with such regularity in names of phony outfits and scam operations.

Others may find it not to their advantage, because the lookup word is unpleasant. The harshness of *cancer*, as in Cancer Society of America, is mitigated by placing it in the middle—American Cancer Society—creating a softening, euphemistic effect.

Is a word in the name actually misleading? Is it a word used so often by insiders that they have lost track of its perception by outsiders? I belonged to an inventors' club a number of years ago. We gradually tumbled to the fact that inventors were not necessarily seen as the noble, praiseworthy human beings we imagined ourselves to be. To many, especially in the media, inventors were either Edison-type, creative geniuses, or kooky, oddball Rube Goldbergs, easy to stereotype and ridicule. We began using the term "product developer."

The club name was, is, Inventors' Workshop International, known by the easy-to-remember, easy-to-say, abbreviation I.W.I. The idea is to help convert amateur inventors into successful professionals. I had a problem with *workshop*, which was accurate enough. But what was the connotation to an outsider? Is it not amateur, bringing to mind the proverbial basement, back yard, or workshop inventor? I should prefer Inventors International.

Of course, if the nonprofit, like any other organization, has a ponderous name, it will be abbreviated in one way or another.

Eventually a nickname, slogan, or abbreviation can become the official name. March of Dimes. You might wish to review Chapter II-1, checking to make sure the abbreviations and nicknames work to your advantage.

Have you heard of Hug a Tree? It is a safety program for children who find themselves lost in the woods (and other places, I guess). Here is a name, a slogan, and the essence of the idea—do not run, stay put, let them find you—rolled into one. Three little words kids can understand, remember, and, most importantly, act upon when frightened and confused. Hug a Tree is my kind of nonprofit name.

Other examples of short, message-laden, nonprofit names: Jerry's Kids, Loaves and Fishes, Goodwill Industries, Right to Life, I Have a Dream Foundation, Hemlock Society.

"Remember that a man's name is to him the sweetest and most important sound in any language." *Dale Carnegie*

II - 16
Field of Dreams - Evoking Emotion and the Senses

Definition: Strong feelings.

Comment: Often a plus.

Examples: Victoria's Secret women's clothing, A Safe Place counseling service, Carnival Cruise Lines.

A few years back, I heard a talk by Jerry Wilson, inventor and manufacturer of the famous Soloflex exercise machines. His marketing breakthrough, he said, came when he realized that while his competitors were selling piles of metal, fancy machinery, he was selling "beautiful birthday suits." He concluded that he was not in the exercise business, a multimillion-dollar industry, but in the cosmetic business, a *multibillion*-dollar industry. So he devised the now-famous advertisements in *Playboy* magazine showcasing sculptured young hunks with birthday suits beyond the reach of most of us, no matter how hard we solo or flex. But we can dream. And that is what it is all about.

Soloflex, the name? Terrific! While it may not make a direct emotional pitch, I would suggest it does so indirectly, subtly, by being ever so appropriate for its task, playing to the persistent dream, to "get back into shape again," the male equivalent of the female's endless quest for "beauty." (Which is not to say women do not use the machine, because they do.)

Automobile manufacturers are master emotion manipulators. Buying a car for transportation purposes only went out with Henry Ford and the Model T. Some of the emotions, or emotional hot buttons, pushed by car dealers: Newest, latest model. "Wait till they see that parked in my driveway." Superiority, achievement, conspicuous wealth. "Won't she be impressed when I drive by." Power, speed, testosterone. "Mine has 350 horsepower, and yours has only 200." Luxury; the living room on wheels. "Power locks, air, tinted glass, leather seats, tilt wheel.... Loaded! The works!"

Extreme examples of the power of these emotional drives are not difficult to come by; everybody has their favorites. Here is one of mine:

A dentist bought his wife a very expensive, fashionable, four-wheel-drive vehicle to use around town. I will not mention the brand name, but it was the ultimate "in its class" (auto ad lingo). The only problem was, something was always going wrong. It was *always* in the shop. After months of hassle, she ran out of patience, and insisted on another vehicle, one that just worked. Anything but that one. He stalled, agonized, and finally relented, buying her the "lesser" brand. Did he dump the prestigious, but nonfunctioning, lemon? No, he had it towed home and parked conspicuously in his driveway to continue to impress the neighbors.

Like all tricks in naming, playing to a customer's emotions is both simple and complex. Is it really just an extension of the suggestion technique?

No list can be complete, but here are a few emotional appeals— what people *really* want—in no particular order:

1. Security: physical safety, living expenses assured, food, shelter, clothing, transportation.

2. Convenience: save time and effort.

3. To feel important: fame, notoriety, position.

4. Power: success, money and what it will buy.

5. Health: body, clean environment, food, air, water.

6. To be well liked: family, friends, work, meet new people.

7. To feel attractive: vanity, glamour, beauty.

8. To belong, to be loyal to, to be involved with: peer group, church,

country, community, school, college, work, cause, charity, club, team.

9. To be physically comfortable: home, furnishings, automobile, luxury, leisure, serenity.

10. Sexual satisfaction: real or vicarious.

11. Adventure, excitement, competition: actual or vicarious.

12. Aesthetic enrichment: art, music, entertainment, collectibles, possessions, travel, beautiful natural surroundings.

13. Acquire knowledge: books, courses, travel, conversation, television, magazines, computers.

14. Something for nothing: gambling, free, bargain.

15. Spiritual: God, worship, hereafter.

16. Nostalgia: history, antiques, family tree.

17. Animals: love of pets.

18. To be young again: beauty aids, sports, games, exercise, memorabilia.

19. Winning: actual or association with winners.

To work an emotional charge into your name, first isolate the most important one. The exercise is similar to writing advertising copy, where you attempt to list the most important buyer benefits first. Play them loud and clear up front. Do not bury them deep in the copy. How much more up-front can you get than in a name?

Sometimes this may be difficult, so you may resort to a euphemistic approach. That is, ignoring the negative, and concentrating on perhaps a contrived emotional positive—such as calling financial protection in case of untimely death "life insurance." Sometimes the

FDA says a name goes too far, as it did with Citrus Hill Fresh Choice orange juice. Since it was made from orange concentrate, they could not use "fresh." Fair enough.

A few more examples of names suggesting an emotional play: Holiday Inns, Cheers bar of TV fame, Guiltless Gourmet potato chips, Grandma's Table restaurant, Cimarron canned chili, White Spot diners, Snuggle Sack, Papyrus paper franchise, Amway products, Northern Lights kayak expeditions, Venetzia Italian foods, Career Track seminars and tapes, Daisy Kingdom fabric store, Safeco Insurance Company.

The Love Boat, Jolly Time popcorn, Fish On boat accessories, Sternwheeler Press, Leaps and Bounds playground by McDonald's, Irish Spring soap, Spray Sensations shower heads, CheZoom custom Chevy hot rod ("...starts like a bomb detonating"), Wholesome and Hearty Foods, Don't Get Mad, Get Smart security systems, Christmas Stocking Fund, Slender Centers, Hawaiian Punch, Dawn soap, Breeze detergent, American Harvest dehydrators.

Never present your name on a dirty business card.

II - 17

Clementine's Drapery Emporium - Names from Song and Story

Comment: Very effective. Ready-made recognition.

Examples: April Showers bridal shop, Gatsby's pub, Secondhand Rose resale clothing.

Aunt Jemima's name for the pancake mix was taken from a popular song of the time, 1889. Chiquita brand bananas came from a radio jingle written for United Fruit Company in 1944. "I'm Chiquita Banana and I've come to say...." (Or something like that.)

The popularization of Cracker Jack took place in reverse. Cracker Jack was a slang expression of the Gay Nineties, meaning okay, or first rate. The popcorn confection's makers reputedly adopted it when someone told them the product was "Cracker Jack." It was fixed in American lore forever with the line "Buy me some peanuts and Cracker Jack" in the song "Take Me Out to the Ball Game."

While we are deviating from our true purpose, another name-to-song, instead of song-to-name, example, is Atchison, Topeka and Santa Fe Railroad, named in 1868. This super-euphonic name with the just-right beat (if you add a *the*) just had to be put into a song—which it was, in the 1946 musical *The Harvey Girls.*

I have said this before, but will say it again: watch out for copyrighted material. Stick to the old standards, preferably written before the turn of the century, even though their meaning to younger people may be limited. Music is one of the most carefully monitored forms of artistic expression, and using even a couple of key words from a song can be grounds for an infringement lawsuit. Newer material, the Beatles songs, for instance, are still in copyright. If you want to name your new tavern the Yellow Submarine, run the idea past your lawyer.

Here are a few more examples of trade and product names from song and story. (More in Chapter II-21, "Humor and Wordplay"):

Seize the Day personal organizer software, Cheshire Cat wine store, Grape Expectations wine store, Scarlet Ribbons fashion shows, King Com fax and communications software, Sherlock Homes real estate (owner's surname was Sherlock), A Place in the Sun tanning parlor, Chimney With Care chimney cleaning, The Real Mother Goose gallery, Almost Heaven hot tubs, Loaves and Fishes.

Taverns and restaurants: Two Beers Before the Blast, Danny Deever's, Aesop's Table, Blazing Salads, Wok Around the Clock, Moby Nick's seafood, Digger O'Dell's, 4 and 20 Blackbirds, Godfather's pizza, Last Hurrah, Tortilla Flats, Walrus and the Carpenter's, Walter Mitty's, Bogart's Joint, Call of the Wild, Barbie's Inferno, Our Daily Bread, Ezekiel's Wheel, Poor Richard's, Last Laugh Comedy Club, Modern Times, Rimski-Korsakoffee House, Irish Eyes tavern.

The Company Store, Brother's Keeper genealogy software, Aladdin thermos bottles, Paper Moon bookstore, Almost Heaven hot tubs, Orient Express and Baker Street mystery bookstores, Secondhand Prose used books, Field of Dreams sports memorabilia, Something Blue and Stitch in Time used clothing, Thunder Road beverages, Oil Can Henry's quick oil change, Confucius Says Chinese food home delivery.

One of my all-time favorites is Glorious Food, a haute New York City catering service, from the song in the play and movie *Oliver*. Tough to improve upon this one.

The Saucerer's Apprentice restaurant, Little Rascals Child Center, Sweet Georgia Brown's restaurant and lounge, Hi Ho Silver, Paper Chase recycling, Jellystone campgrounds, Diamond Lill's antique jewelry, Clothes Encounters, 52 Pickup carry home cuisine, Little House day-care center, Gasoline Alley antiques.

The Happy Hooker boat mooring hook, Twice Told Tales used-book store, Charley Chan's restaurant, Pooh Corner Educare, Inc., End of the Trail secondhand store, Alice's Looking Glass beauty salon, Red Hen pantry, Long John Silver's restaurants, *This Old House* television show, Antiques On My Mind, Ladies In Red commercial ladybug sales, Phobe Snow lounge, Casey Jones Junction tavern.

The Enchanted Florist, Hill Street Booze tavern, Barnum and Bagel, I Am Woman hair salon, Wells Cargo auto roof carrier, Let Them Eat Cake bakery, Guys and Dolls hair design, I Love a Mystery bookstore, A Tisket a Taskett gift baskets, Gentle Persuasion lounge, Silver Lining garbage bags.

Able to Cane chair repairs, I Love Juicy juice bar, My Kind of Town tours of Chicago, Mrs. Robinson's hair salon, P.S. I Love You gift shop, Cafe Ba-Ba-Reeba, My Fair Lady beauty parlor, Indiana Joan's clothing store, Blazing Paddles whitewater tours.

Naming is too important to be left to generals.

II - 18
Trite and True - The Lighthearted Side of Naming

Having plowed through the hundreds of previous examples, you have probably developed a finely tuned eye for the clever and imaginatively crafted name. In the following four chapters, creativity is pushed to the limit, and, in some cases, beyond. Of course, most of you will not find these techniques applicable to your situation. But I hope you will enjoy reading about them anyway.

The great thing about lighthearted naming is, you have no problem deciding if your CPS is a candidate. If you run a professional office? No way. A neighborhood fruit and vegetable market? No way. Any serious business? No way.

Or is that true in this day and age?

Be extra careful when you test lighthearted (or lightheaded) names for your own use. Please, not only conduct all the tests in Chapter I-16 to the best of your ability, but add the aforementioned one-week waiting period test. What many of these names lack is staying power. After the initial rush, the chuckle, the "Isn't that great!" many are quite forgettable. They require too many mental jumps. They do not fit logically into the disinterested stranger's easy recall frame of reference. By waiting a bit you will also be able to ponder the "Are they laughing with me or laughing at me?" question.

That said, what businesses use this technique most frequently— that is, humor, whimsy, plays on words, the rest? Generally: bookstores (volumes of material), hair and nail salons (but very few barbershops), resale and secondhand stores, gift and card shops, taverns and bars (and, to a lesser extent, restaurants), antique shops, boutiques, publishers (compelled to be clever), tourist shopsies, and many other personal service businesses. You get the idea.

II - 19
For Jerks Only - Negative and Self-Deprecatory Names

Definition: "Diminishing in value. Disparaging; belittling."

Comment: Long shot.

Examples: Faux Pas, Inc., Dog's Breath restaurant, Little Charm motel.

Every good-sized city has a newspaper that prints legal notices or notices of record: who is suing whom, major property sales, bankruptcies, divorces, calls for bids, and new business licenses taken out. Scanning the new biz column each week is a good way to get a feel for the naming trends in your area, at least among start-ups. Doing so in my town, I make two observations: In many attempts at self-deprecatory whimsy or humor, it is amazing how often the message coming through is not the humor, but that the owner does not take his or her business seriously. I found Oops Poops Company. I mean, really! Do you expect the Oops Poops Company to be in business next month? The other: It is amazing how many give no clue as to what they are about, what they do (aside from creating stupid names). I am talking fifty percent or more. Oops Poops. What do they do? I have no idea. And I do not care. Onward.

I have always had a problem with self-deprecatory names like Radio Shack. Shack? (The name has never stopped me from patronizing the stores, however.) An analogy would be in giving a speech. You never open with an apology. But you cannot argue with success. I grant one thing, it is very distinctive and memorable. Perhaps it conveys the perfect cachet. Anyway, they certainly like it. A few years back, they sued an outfit calling itself Auto Shack, forcing a change to Auto Zone.

Pizza Hut. Reputedly, the early owners, the Crowley brothers, decided the lookup word, pizza, had to be in the name. Cannot blame them for that. And they had a sign with only nine spaces. That left room for three letters and a space between the words. Their building looked like a run-down shanty of sorts. So.... Obviously, in hindsight, it works, conveying a friendly, informal place to enjoy pizza.

I would suggest, however, that for every winner, like Radio Shack and Pizza Hut, there may be many names using the technique that do not pass muster. Handle with care. The idea in business is to make a positive impression, is it not?

Nevertheless, here are some winners and losers, each good for a twitch of the cheek:

For Brats Only children's hair stylists, the Ugly Stepsister salon, Somewhat Ltd. Productions, Blockhead Media, Rusty Scupper restaurant, Filthy McNasty's tavern, Toad in the Hole typing service. Old Weird Harold's Nostalgia, Poor Taste camp clothing, Rent A Wreck (actually quite accurate), Looney Tunes sporting goods, Chili Bordello restaurant, and Stinker gas stations (with a cute skunk logo).

World's Wurst restaurants, Not For Sissies bar, Mud Pie Enterprises, Blimpie Industries, Evil People lounge, Dilettante Chocolates, Garbage—The Practical Journal for the Environment, Awful Brothers gas stations, BigmOuth Software, Scuzzi and Bub City restaurant, Wet Dreams water sports.

II - 20
How 'Bout Them Jumbo Shrimp - Oxymorons and Oxy-like Names

Definition: A figure of speech in which incongruous or contradictory terms are combined. From Greek *oxumoros*, pointedly foolish.

Comment: Pointedly foolish.

Examples: Lowe Alpine, Steel Magnolias, Intimate Strangers, True Lies.

This tongue-in-cheek, or perhaps foot-in-mouth, technique could possibly be called For Taverns and Road Houses Only, because they seem to be the most common users. No problem here, except some strike me as downright crude, two disparate words simply shoved together. Plaid Rabbit, Wooden Chicken. That, of course, is intended. For some reason, Stone Balloon tickles my funny bone a lot more. I also like New York's Cellar in the Sky. Because there is no official list of oxymorons that I am aware of, they are not covered in Part III. And keep in mind, as with any form of attempted humor, what is funny to one person may be ultra-unfunny to another. Military intelligence, bankers trust, civil service. Oxys are what you make of them.

Descendants of early Oregon settlers, the ones who survived the rigors of the Oregon Trail in the 1840s, soon assumed a self-proclaimed nobility of priority, akin to coming over on the *Mayflower*. Today, some refer to them facetiously as ox-cart aristocrats. (Maybe it should be oxy-cart aristocrats.) Two local Mexican restaurants have used the technique: Machismo Mouse, healthy Mexican food, and Chez José (Chez, connoting high-class French). I received a gift from Australia, a boomerang manufactured by Stones Throw Boomerang Company. A name that is probably not meant to be an oxymoron, but seems like one, is Tall Grass Technology. It is a breath of fresh air off the Great Plains, because it sets itself apart from the thousands of techie-sounding, me-too computer company names.

Here are a few oxymoronish examples to get you started, if you are so inclined. Some were found in *Jumbo Shrimp & Other Almost Perfect Oxymorons*, by Warren S. Blumenfeld, Ph.D. Others were picked up here and there.

Beggar's banquet, cheerful tortoise, deliberate speed, idiot savant, working vacation, freezer burn, civil war, first annual, global village, exact estimate, casual elegance, pretty ugly, serious humor, little giant, same difference, original copy, balanced budget, idle curiosity, weather forecast, iron butterfly, lonely crowd, sad clown, gentleman farmer, tentative conclusion.

Deafening silence, icy hot, fatal cure, genuine fake, pointed circle, waking dreams, executive cowboy, rusty pelican, wise fools, soft anvil, hot Siberia, soft gold, instant classic.

Add a few from *Romeo and Juliet*: Brawling love, loving hate, heavy lightness, serious vanity, feather of lead, bright smoke, cold fire, sick health.

Hundreds of rose varieties.
Which name comes to mind first?

II - 21
Cruel and Unusual Punishment - Humor and Wordplay

Definition: Pun — a play on words, sometimes in a different sense of the same word, sometimes on the similar sense or sound of different words.

Comment: Okay, under the right circumstances.

Examples: Custard's Last Stand, Dear John sanitary service, Nice To Be Kneaded massage therapy center.

Are there any rules here? Hardly.

All of the example names attempt to catch your eye, stop your eye, gain your attention with the clever, the funny, the outrageous. They attempt to convey lack of pretention, friendliness, a place to relax and enjoy, or a casual business to patronize. They invite you in.

Although this is a wonderfully entertaining technique, I must restate my stuffy warning: these names may not be as memorable as their creators believe them to be. Many, it seems to me, do not have the staying power of a less jocular appellation. Others may be too clever, not enough people get it.

Attempting to pigeonhole the examples below as this or that is not worth the trouble. Some are perhaps misplaced oxymorons or are self-deprecatory. Some are simply names that caught my eye. And some are, in my opinion, really bad. But still, they caught my eye. Enjoy.

M.Y.O.B. business accounting software, Flatt Tire Company, China Clipper hair styling, StowAways food-storage containers, Ash Kickers chimney cleaners, Jack the Ribber, Hamburger Patti's, Watts My Line electrical contractor, Marquis de Sod landscaping, Prehysterical toy animals, John Barleycorn Memorial Pub.

Pig Out barbecue, Fuddrucker's restaurants, Witches Brew tavern, Brown Bag software, Aromadillos herb-filled pillows, Legal Ease software, Fiasco restaurant, The Sly Fox, Speedy Gonzales Mexican food, Tomaine Tommy's, Fat City cafe, Flakey Jake's, Chuck E. Cheese, Porkey's barbecue, Out to Lunch, Queenie's Weenies.

Franks for the Memories, Apparels of Pauline's dress shop, Your Place or Mine, Tanks a Lot water tanks, Something's Fishy, T.G.I. Friday's, Fit to be Tried ear-plugs, Just Desserts bakery, Lewis N. Clark travel accessories, Chips Ahoy cookies, Duck Tape (the way people pronounce duct tape), HiQ computer company.

L'Eggs pantyhose, Veritable Quandary bar, Wuxtry award for headline writing (from the turn-of-the-century newsboy's cry), Deep Thought computer (porno movie *Deep Throat*), Market Fax stock market newsletters by fax, Auld Lang Sign Company, Dental Ben (*Gentle Ben* book series), 24 Carrot Cakes bakery, The Blind Alley Venetian blind company.

X-Cargo automobile rooftop travel container, Miami Voice voice mail system, Big Bin storage bins, Dog-Eared Publications, Boondocks restaurant, Quick and Dirty signs, Pork Barrel Press, Hung Far Low Chinese restaurant (means "almond blossom"), Grease Monkey International fast-lube, Eat Your Heart Out restaurant, The Clip Joint hair salon.

A few years ago, two magazines came out devoted to environmental concerns, *Garbage* and *Buzzworm*. Based on the names alone, however you classify them, humorous or simply attention-getting, I predicted early failure. I was wrong. They are, happily, still around, proving serendipity often lurks behind the trash can or compost pile. Buzzworm, by the way, is an old-time word for rattlesnake, thus the warning before environmental disaster strikes.

Continuing:

Witt's End tavern, Fickle Fingers nail salon, A Woman's Place feminist bookstore, Chocolate Moose coffee-house, Bridal Sweet, Den of Antiquity antiques, Eastern Onion singing telegrams, Elmer Fudge, Arche Rival computer company, Ill Eagle fireworks, Madcap Enterprises, Hot Lips pizza, Stanley Steamer carpet cleaning, Our

Weigh weight-control center.

Deck the Walls wallpaper, The Mac Factor, Maid Right maid service, Grin and Wear It, Haute Dogs, Seams Right alteration shop, Sir Plus clothing, Catbird Seat bookstore, P's & Q's secretarial service, Wise Acres herb and flower farm, Current Designs kayaks, McDivots golf equipment, New Conceptions, Inc., surrogate parenting.

Present Perfect gift shop, Rubbermaid, Title Wave bookstore, Cache 22 data-compression software, Mindsweeper early morning coffee, Safe Six, Hot Off The Press publishing, Hooked on Phonics, From Rocks to Riches lapidary shop, The Whole Nine Yards fabric shop, Eclectricity gifts, Planned Parrothood.

Junk and Disorderly used furniture, Lox, Stock and Bagel, Acute cafe, Funny Farm restaurant, Genghis Cohen's restaurant, Sacred Cow restaurant, Queen Bea's, Down the Hatch, Eggs Cetera, Souper Salad, Lox a Luck, Something's Fishy, The Brick Shirt House, Currier and Chives catering, Bug Off pesticide company, Tank and Tummy gas and grub.

"For every man there is something in the vocabulary
that would stick to him like a second skin.
His enemies have only to find it." *Ambrose Bierce*

II - 22
Bloo Skyz Airways - Stylized Spelling

Definition: Stylize: to conform to a particular style.

Comment: Break all the rules and win.

Examples: Kwik Mart, EZ Pik, Pay N Sav, and the rest.

The definition is misleading. We are, of course, talking about deliberate misspelling and abbreviation for attention-grabbing effect.

For years I have used office glue in a bright, yellow tube, never really noticing the name, UHU Stik. One day I actually read it, UHU Stik. What the heck does that mean? A little explanation on the side told me. "Don't say glue—say Yoo-Hoo." Now I know.

Most kooky spellings, as I like to call them, do not have to be explained. In fact many are so overused you wonder if the regular words might work better. Sav, Kwik, EZ. In any event, a few do-it-yourself tips:

Eliminate "unnecessary" vowels. Value to valu, save to sav. N-R-Getic. Substitute soundalikes. New to nu. Endings, sy or ty become z. Ck endings drop one letter or the other. Pic, pik, pac pak, quik, quic. Gh is altered to f, as in Tuff-Kote. Mighty can become MY-TE, as in MY-TE Fine Foods. And the standard twist, and becomes N, as in In N Out market. You becomes U, as in the Reebock slogan, "Reebock Lets U.B.U." Be = B. See = C. Two = 2. Four = 4. New = Nu. The becomes Z, as in Z Best.

Examples:

Dri-Z-air moisture remover, Laycee (lacy) stuff, Tuff Lite flashlights, Redy Coat paint, E-Z (everything), Spred paints, Kwikset locks,

HiJaak Import graphics-importing software, Garlique garlic supplement, Caddylak Publishing Company.

Uneda biscuit is an oldie, along with Kleenex tissues. Lamskin imitation sheepskin seat covers, Krusteaz mixes. One of my favorite names, NeXT computers, was stylized by simply capitalizing non-customary letters. Another would be GEnie, General Electric's on-line e-mail and information service. Very good.

One way to get up to speed in this area of naming is to study the custom (or ego) license plates you see on the road. Here the technique is pushed to the extreme, because the entire message has to fit into a maximum of seven or eight spaces. The great ones are legion, the most famous being, probably, L A LAW. My favorite is DUPA, which I spotted on an Ohio plate. *Dupa* is Polish for rear end.

The following mini-epic poem plays to the attention span, as well as the vernacular, of the sound bite generation, while illustrating a number of "sophisticated" stylized spelling and abbreviation techniques.

KRZN TRU

BBY N BD
HI SKL 2
WANA D8
I LUV U

BIG 4-0
RIDN HI
0 NESTR
GETN BY

FOXY SR
PRLY G8S
C UR LIF
N
EGO PL8S

II - 23
Members Only - Argot and Jargon

Definitions: Argot: a specialized vocabulary or set of idioms used by a particular group. Jargon: the specialized or technical language of a trade, group, or profession.

Comment: Your call.

Examples: The Caddis Nymph, the Monster Lunker, the Greased Line, the Barbless Hook.

What do the above example names mean to you? Okay, *hook* gave it away. They are, or were, names of fly-fishing shops. Fly-fishing, in case you do not know, is the Ivy League of sport fishing. Among the many barriers to membership is a complex insider's jargon.

So, because the shop owner is dealing with a self-styled elite that, in many cases, would like to keep things as closed as possible anyway, and is an avid member himself, he is faced with something of a dilemma. Should the store name speak strongly to the in-group in their beloved lingo? Or should it reach out just a bit to the uninitiated, and invite them in to learn about the sport and spend their money?

It is the old question, harped upon throughout *Names That Sell*, of speaking to strangers. The owner wants to distinguish his shop from the numerous Joe's Sporting Goods stores selling take-out cartons of worms, spinning reels, and camouflage parkas to lowly "meat" fishermen. (In some cases they really do not want to do business with strangers. I have been in fly-fishing shops where the clerks will not speak to you unless they know you.)

On the other hand, perhaps some owners, in selecting a name reeking of exclusivity, do not consider the negative side. Some very nice people might like to outfit themselves at their store if only the name invited them in—like, for instance, in plain English. How about the Avid Angler, or Fly-fishing Fanatics, Ltd., with suitable slogans?

Some activities, however, require initiation, and are just not open to everyone. Gorge Performance is, in my opinion, a nifty name. But what do you think it is about? Answer: they sell sailboarding (or windsurfing) equipment in Portland, Oregon. "Gorge" refers to the Columbia Gorge, where the Columbia River cuts through the Cascade Mountains and the summer winds blow at tremendous speeds. Board sailors from around the world are attracted to the place. They know what and where the "Gorge" is, and, since it is not for beginners, perhaps no one else matters.

I do not want to make a big deal of this—even though I might sound overly sarcastic—as it affects only a few. And I am not asserting that people using these names are always wrong. After all, exclusivity means just that, to exclude. I am just raising the point for thoughtful consideration.

A safe name is sometimes a smart name.

II - 24
All in the Family - Developing a Theme

Definition: Theme: "An implicit or recurrent idea, a motif."

Comment: Often a good strategic move.

Examples: Apple Computers to Macintosh. Elsie the Borden cow's dairy products to Elmer's glue. Honda Accord, with models DX, LX, and EX.

The English-speaking world has used surnames (family, or last names) to show shared, group identity, and first (given) names to distinguish individuals within the group. (Until recently, this formula was more or less automatic, but it seems to be falling apart.) A similar system may be adopted by CPSs for marketing purposes. The advantages are obvious. Take a hard look at this technique as part of your overall marketing strategy.

One of the outstanding name creations of late is Egghead Software. They bill themselves as "North America's Software Eggsperts," and, along with their little egg-shaped "professor" logo, their motif includes: "eggstraspecial values, eggciting upgrades, eggceptional performance." These "eggstraordinary" words are all trademarked, by the way.

PooPets are small sculptures made of cow manure that serve as decorative garden fertilizer dispensers. Or, as they call them, "Friendly, functional, fertilizing, fecal figurines." Are you getting the drift? Each sculpture has a name in keeping with the manure theme: Stool Pigeons, Cow Pie Cows, Turdles, Dung Bunnies, Mini-Poos, Scat Cats, Stool Toads, and a skunk named— what else?—Pepe LaPoo. These imaginative, slightly naughty product names get people's attention and really move the product. Can you get any closer to a nondescript commodity than poo?

Anything that ties the product or service line together with a theme can work. It can have a clever twist, as above, or be as straightforward as coupling the company name with each different product. Every mutual fund "family" does it. Fidelity Magellan, Fidelity Value, Fidelity Equity Income II. Boeing has done it successfully for years with its seven series airplanes: 707, 727, 737, 747, 757, 767, and 777. McDonald's uses all sorts of variations on McTheme: Ronald McDonald, Egg McMuffin, Big Mac. And you can too. No, not with McDonald's name, your name.

Speaking of model names:

Just as I have avoided plunging into the steaming jungle of high fashion and fragrance names, you will notice I have more or less avoided automobile and model names and numbers. Well, I can avoid them no more. The auto makers can teach us many lessons in naming, but sometimes it is difficult to figure out exactly what they are. Consider, on one hand, that the world's auto makers are old pros at naming, the very best. On the other hand, because they have so many cars and models to deal with, and they change so fast, some, especially the model names, can turn out to be pure gibberish to strangers, i.e. you and me.

Automobile names come in five or six parts: family (Ford Motor Company), subsidiary or product (Mercury Division), model (Cougar), model number or designation (XR-7), and year (19XX).

Besides identification, why so complicated?

1. People like choices, even if the differences are sometimes superficial. If Chevrolet offers an array of 179 product and model combinations, the customer is more likely to stick around and choose one Chevrolet or another, and not mosey on down the street to Ford or Honda.

2. It is part of the automobile "culture" and tradition. They have done it for years, and it sells cars.

3. The prattle factor. Fancy names are conversation openers for salespeople and everyone who likes to talk cars.

4. Frequent name and model number changes provide something "new" to sell, even when nothing is actually new except the color. The "new model year" syndrome.

5. Manipulating product and model names increases the likelihood of hitting various buyers' "hot buttons." Some are turned on by whatever they perceive as the newest, the latest. "Got to have it." Economy buyers, the cheapskates, will always opt for the "base" model, no extras, plain Jane. At the other extreme, some people are hopelessly seduced by luxury models. "It only adds $50.00 to the payments."

Like money and grades in school, model designations are subject to inflation. "DL" means deluxe, or, in autospeak, the bottom of the line. "L" means luxury, a smidgeon above. Often they are coupled with "X," because, as we have learned, it is an all-purpose power letter. "Z" is the sporty letter. The very top of the line usually has additional "prestige" letters, numbers, and/or names, such as "LE" for limited edition, or "GT" for grand touring. "S" can mean special or sport, "i" fuel injection, "t" turbo.

Number systems can provide genuinely useful information. For years Volvo used a three-number system, such as 245, meaning two wheel drive, four cylinders, and five doors. Numbers such as 560 or 750 can mean body style or engine capacity.

Are we naming cars? Unlikely. So what are the general lessons for the rest of us?

1. Distinguishing products and services with theme names and numbers is good marketing, if done carefully. People like them, especially if they convey meaningful information.

2. Keep it simple. Do not deliberately confuse with complicated model names and numbers. (Unless your objective is to deliberately confuse.) Series 1000, 2000, and 3000 will often differentiate nicely. Another simple technique is to choose product or model names all beginning with the same letter. Or, as is commonly done, use theme names—birds, cats, zodiac, etc. See Part III.

3. Test and monitor the effect of your model names. Find out if your customers actually "get it." If, after a reasonable amount of time and explanation, they do not, something is wrong. As with any name, rethink and rename.

How Apple Computers Got its Name

The name was chosen, presumably by Steve Jobs, under pressure to finalize partnership papers between him and Stephen Wozniak. Various writers have listed the following as influencing the choice: The Beatles record label. (Jobs was a Beatles fan, especially of John Lennon.) Jobs ate a fruit diet and had recently picked apples in Oregon. He also wanted a name that would appear before Atari in the telephone book. Finally, he felt everyone liked apples.

Other interesting tie-ins, intended or not: The apple is the fruit of knowledge. (An early logo attempt showed Isaac Newton under his apple tree.) Adam and Eve and the apple, signifying first, and Apple, one of the first truly personal computers. Apples are associated with school—apple for the teacher, apple polisher. (Interesting also in light of Apple computer's dominance in the educational market.) Play on the word *byte,* as in "Byte into an Apple," an early slogan. And Apple's longtime logo, showing a bite out of an incongruously, rainbow-colored apple. As an added bonus, the name Apple led easily into a family of product names, such as Macintosh and Newton.

That Apple was friendly, nonthreatening and nontechnical-sounding, at a time, 1976, when almost all computer-related names were the opposite, is very important. Though Apple computers were breakthrough products, and would have succeeded whatever they were called, one cannot help thinking the name was a factor in their astonishing success.

II - 25
Amalgamated Buggy Whip - When and How to Change a Name

Comment: Make sure it is not just change for the sake of change.

Examples: Kentucky Fried Chicken to KFC, American Can Company to Primerica, Kresge to Kmart

Do you recall the uproar when Coca-Cola changed its sacrosanct beverage formula? Regular Coke was soon reinstated as Coca-Cola Classic. The old name, Coke, named the new Pepsi-like Coke. Or was it the other way around? I have never understood whether all of this was a corporate fiasco, a genuine blunder, or a shrewdly planned attention-getting ploy. Regardless, it remains one of the most controversial product and name changes of the decade. Does the Coke name change hold a lesson for us? Probably not. They play in a different league.

When should you consider a name change?

1. While reading *NTS* it dawns on you that the name you have been using all these years was never that good in the first place. It is not doing its job. Please do not get defensive about a name just because it has been around for a long time and you have so much invested in it. A bad name is a bad name.

2. Your company, product, or service has outgrown its name. It does not accurately reflect what the company does, current technology, or the image you wish to project. You have not manufactured, say, buggy whips in years. But you do manufacture or sell dozens of products and services, impossible to reflect in a narrow identifier name. One of my favorite changes of this sort is Cincinnati Milling Machine Corp. to Cincinnati Milicron.

Kentucky Fried Chicken abbreviated to initials, KFC Corp. (Remember, powerful, established corporations can get away with this.) I suspect it was done at the insistence of the board of directors, who did not want to be thrown in jail by the food police. Even though I try to avoid fried foods, the word "fried" in the name did not bother me. Maybe it was just familiarity, but I thought the old name had jolly good cadence.

3. There has been, or will be, a change in ownership—merger, sale, takeover, etc.

What to do:

First the easy one, mergers and takeovers. If a smaller business is absorbed into a larger one, the company name will, in almost all cases, change. It is a matter of dominance and power, big fish swallows little fish. "And we'll keep everything, including the name, exactly as it is," is corporatespeak for "Everything will change within a month." In most cases, however painful, this is as it should be.

Of course, the product and service names involved in the takeover are a different matter. A significant chunk of the purchase price was for the trademarks. Still, itchy minds may find it difficult to resist tampering. What will be, will be.

The sale of a small business, where it will continue to be operated in, say, the same location, doing somewhat the same things, is another matter, posing difficult name problems.

This is especially true if the business name embodies the former owner's name. If the name rights were not included in the sale, or other agreement reached, it must be changed. If the name was included, what to do?

Obviously there are no firm rules. Except one. Slow down. It is instinctive for a new owner to wish to put his or her imprimatur on a business, especially if he or she paid a lot of money for it.

I always wonder when I drive down the street and see a banner hanging on a business reading, "Under New Management," often accompanied by a new name. Has the proud New Management really thought about the message it conveys? Just because new people are running the place, should we assume it will be better run? What was so bad about the Old Management? If it was so bad, why did people go there all along? Does this "New Management" mean the old customers should stop patronizing the establishment, deferring to the onrush of enlightened new patrons, because their judgment over the years is branded deficient?

No simple answer to the above, but I hope the analogy will make you stop and consider. I have observed many local and neighborhood businesses change hands. Some prosper. Others stumble, and gradually slide into oblivion. It could be my imagination, and there is no way to prove it, but hasty, ill-considered name changes seem to accompany the latter.

Before discussing techniques for smooth name changes, let us look at a few examples, some successful, some not:

In the 1920s, Carl Widman started buying up local bus companies with the idea of incorporating them into a regional or nationwide line. One 1922 purchase was the Greyhound Line of Muskegon, Michigan. Widman thought the suggestive name, along with the great logo, was the best of the bunch, and began using it on all the buses.

Up in the northern end of New York state there is a wonderful museum that used to be called the Thousand Islands Shipyard Museum. To me, the name was confusing. (As well as intriguing, to a boat lover like myself.) Turns out it was an insider's name (that stranger thing again), referring to the location (the Thousand Islands section of the St. Lawrence River), the primary boats in the collection, (St. Lawrence skiffs), and the museum's site (an old shipyard). Now it is called the Antique Boat Museum, a good example of a two-birds-with-one-stone name change—accurately reflecting the expanded scope of the collection, antique, wooden power-and sailboats, and getting rid of some confusing information, "shipyard."

In Georgia, one of the old-line banks was known for years as the Fulton National Bank (Fulton being the county Atlanta is in). A few years ago they changed to Bank of the South, reflecting, I suppose, an expanded area of operations. Now it is BankSouth, an inevitable combination, smacking, perhaps, of trendiness. Bank of the South was good enough for me. One thing in their favor, however, they were not one of the hundreds of savings and loan associations scrambling around to get those scandal-tainted words out of their names and, in the early 1990s, often precipitating complete identity crises.

We have seen how Darkie toothpaste was changed to Darlie to remove offensive connotations. Some other name changes to improve the image: Rapeseed oil to canola oil, hake fish to Pacific whiting, and Hospice House to Hopewell House. Every once in a while a European breakfast cereal called muesli surfaces in the U.S. To me, the name connotation is mucilage. A good candidate for a change. Years back the U.S. Bureau of Revenue changed its name to the more euphemistically correct Internal Revenue Service. Before that, the U.S. Department of War changed its name to the somewhat more accurate Department of Defense.

Here is a great marketing name change: Hog Island to Paradise Island (presumably to turn it into a paradise of wall-to-wall condominiums). Those old-timers had no class. In a similar vein, out in eastern Oregon, in the old days, a few ladies set up in tents and shacks each fall to entertain the cowpokes at roundup time. The place became known as, what else?, Whorehouse Meadow. (Someone must have read Chapter II-8, "Just Say It.") In the 1960s, during a spasm of sanitizing zeal, the government agency overseeing the land changed its maps to read Naughty Girl Meadow. Happy to report, after protests by those interested in historical correctness, the true name was eventually restored. Now, down by the Columbia River, near where I live, there is a landmark called Rooster Rock. But that is not what the early waterborne namesmiths called it.

With so many cities, towns, and regions going after the tourist buck, they are paying attention to their names. Baker, Oregon, located at a strategic point on the old Oregon Trail, is heavily into luring cash-laden visitors. Its old name was Baker City, but for years the post office would not accept two-word names (unless, I guess, you were New York), so it was just Baker, not too exciting a name. Lately, the P.O. relented, and they changed it back. I think it lends an old-time flavor, harking back to the days when folks were given to facetiously naming one-street, western towns "City"—when they were anything but.

Vancouver, Washington, is confused by some with the much larger West Coast city, Vancouver, British Columbia, Canada. So, the citizens, some years back, voted on whether to restore its very old, historic name, Fort Vancouver. It did not pass, but they came up with a good compromise, Vancouver, U.S.A. Hey, remember when the citizens of North Dakota considered dropping *North*, because they worried visitors were staying away because of the suggestion of cold weather. The vote to change failed, but it shows that someone was thinking about marketing and speaking to strangers. Suggestive names can suggest the *wrong* things, too. Even an entire country can wonder. The proper name of Mexico is United Mexican States. Now there is a hot debate going on over changing to just Mexico, which everybody calls it anyway, to differentiate from the United States of America.

Rippling River resort near Mt. Hood, Oregon, changed its name to the Resort at the Mountain. Why? Because, in spite of the nifty, alliterative name, they finally had to admit there was no river nearby, rippling or otherwise. I have mentioned United Airlines' aborted change to Allegis Corp. About the same time, Continental Illinois Bank changed to CONILL—and back. This may be twenty-twenty hindsight, but I would modestly suggest that had someone involved read *Names That Sell* they might have avoided that one. A successful change of the same vintage was Consolidated Foods Corporation's change to Sara Lee Corp., adopting their lead trademark as trade name.

How to go about changing trade names in use:

1. **Test** before you leap. Besides passing all the regular tests in Chapter I-16, the new name must be a real improvement over the one you have.

2. **Costs**. Consider the cost of the name change. The larger the company, the more expensive it will be. Get some hard figures. You will have to make up your own checklist, but remember, it can go far beyond letterheads, envelopes, and business cards.

3. **Customers**. Have you considered your customers? Will a new name be perceived as a slap in the face? (Under New Management.) Will it cause confusion? Does the name change cut the customer loose, in effect, breaking his or her habit patterns? "What's going on there? Might as well start looking around." If your business provides

staple-type goods or basic services, have you considered how thankful people are just to find a place that simply does a good job, day in, day out—one less hassle in their lives. They will reward you with steady patronage and all-important word-of-mouth advertising. But what happens to the word of mouth when you junk the name they love, yes, love, and trust?

4. **Fads**. There is an almost irresistible urge to shorten trade names, to acronymize them, to render them unintelligible. Sometimes this works—Cincinnati Milicron, AMF Industries—sometimes not— Allegis, CONILL. Again, do not forget that fads and trends sweep the country from time to time. Often, the more aware, with-it, and energetic a person is, the more, not less, likely he or she is to be caught up in them. The trap of presumed cleverness is difficult to resist. About two-thirds of corporate name changes involve shortening.

5. **Avoid** meaningless names unless you really know what you are doing. Again, see Chapter II-2, "Initials." Some meaning, continuity, or recognition is almost always desirable.

6. **Do it**. Once a decision to change a name has been made, it is probably best to change immediately, get it over with. There are, however, ways to upgrade a name short of complete change, or work it into use over a period of time. A few:

a. Adopt a slogan to follow the name, incorporating the gist of the new message. If Bannard Farms, a produce grower, plans to shift into growing for the specialty shop and high-class restaurant market, it might follow the name with "Specialty food products for restaurants and hotels," "Select Produce," or "Gourmet Vegetables." I love slogans and favor their use for many other reasons, but a complete discussion is beyond the scope of this book.

b. The slogan can, should, contain words that will eventually become the new name. Bannard Select Foods.

c. Or, go directly to the new name and follow with the standard changeover statement, "formerly Bannard Farms"—although in this example it is probably not necessary.

d. Use both old and new names, gradually reducing the emphasis on the old one till it fades out of existence. Bannard Farms/Bannard Select Foods. Or form a new division with a new name.

Although the above examples illustrate some of the often-used, toe-in-the-water methods, you can see the results leave something to be desired. Even with the little information we have in this hypothetical case, the situation cries out for something more imaginative, at least of the caliber of Gallo wine's upgrade to Ernest and Julio Gallo (very smooth). Bannard, I would suggest, might go further. It is a perfect candidate for a change to a new trademark.

"There is only negative equity in a bad name. When the name is bad, things tend to get worse. When the name is good, things tend to get better." *Al Ries and Jack Trout*

A Few Attention-Grabbing Names

Atomic Fireball jawbreaker candy
Mr. Zog's Original Sex Wax ("The best for your stick.")
Coffin Nail cigarettes
Krazy Glue
Charley perfume
Amazing Goop adhesives
Dog's Breath restaurant

PART III - LISTS

III - 1
Latin and Greek

This is an arbitrary selection of Latin words I find particularly pleasing to the eye and ear, followed by the Greek alphabet. As Latin is an English root language, you will find many meaningful words and word parts. And, of course, you will recognize many that have been used in business names. Definitions are not given, as it is more interesting to ponder the words, savor their sounds, and figure them out. If, however, you decide to use a word or part, be certain to check, even if you have to track it down in a standard English dictionary. *Domus*, for instance, will be found under *domestic* or *domicile*. The Latin roots are *domesticus*, *domicilium* and *domus*, all relating to the house.

acer, adeo, alo, altus, ambitio, ambulo, amicus, amor, Aprilis, aqua, arbor, auctor, audacia, audio, Augustus, aureus

bonus, Brittannia

caelestis, caesar, carmen, conservo, corona, creo, cultura

December, decor, delecto, dignus, disco, domus, dulcis, duro, dux

equis, ergo, extra

facile, familia, femina, fidelis, finis, fortis, fortuna, forum

gladius, gloria, gusto

honor

imperator, industria, intellego, intelligentia, inventor, invictus, Iulius, Iunius

Janus, Julius

laudis, lego, lex, liber, libertas, luna, lupus, luxuria

magnus, Maia, manus, Martius, mellis, memoria, mirus, modus

navis, November, novis

obduro, October, opis, optimus, opus, orbis

patria, pax, pecunia, perfectur, premo, prudentia, publicus, purus

quantus, quid

regis, resisto, rota

salsus, salutis, scientia, September, signum, silva, simplex, sine, sol, stella, summa, supra

tantus, terra, Troia

velox, veni, veritas, vesper, victor, victoria, vida, vidi, vigor, villa, vici, volo, voluptas, vox

Greek: Alpha (first), beta, gamma, delta (triangle), epsilon, zeta, eta, theta, iota, kappa, lambda, mu, nu, xi, omicron, pi, rho, sigma, tau, upsilon, phi, chi, psi, omega (great, the end).

III - 2
Ancient and Mythological

This list is an amalgam of ancient and ancient-sounding words. They come from the Bible, legend, literature, mythology, and geography. No particular distinction is made between, say, Greek, Roman, or Nordic mythology, because, when used in a name, it is not that important (as long as it is checked beforehand). To the receiver of the name, it is the initial impression that counts, a signal of recognition. The namesmith is looking for words or word parts that are appropriate, that sound right.

As with the Latin list, this is far from academic. You will recognize many business, product, and service names and name parts herein—such as Nike sports shoes and apparel, Ajax cleanser, and Hercules powder. Hopefully, you will find something that will give your name a truly creative spin, as opposed to, for example, the overused "Viking."

Achilles, Adam, Adonais, Aero, Agamemnon, Ajax, Alexander, Alexandria, Amazon, Andromeda, Aphrodite, Apollo, Aquila, Arcadia, Argonaut, Argus, Aries, Arion, Artemis, Asura, Atlanta, Athena, Athenae, Athens, Atlantis, Atlas, Aurora, Avalon, Aztec

Babylon, Bacchus, Byzantium

Calypso, Calibur, Calliope, Camilla, Carthage, Cassius, Centaur, Chimaera, Circe, Cleopatra, Corinth, Corinthian, Cupid, Cyclops, Cygnus

Delphi, Delphinus, Diana, Dolphin, Doric

Earth, Echo, Egypt, Eldorado, Electra, Elysian Plain, Elysium, Eros, Ethiopia, Europa, Evander, Eve

Gemini, genius, Golden Fleece, Goliath, Gordian knot, griffin

Hector, Helen, Helios, Hercules, Hermes, Hero, Homer, Hydra

Icarus, Ida, Illiad, Io, Ionia, Iria, Iris, Island of the Sun, Isis, Ithaca

Jason, Jonah, Jove, Juno, Jupiter

Laurel, leprechaun, leviathan, Liberia, lotus, Luna, Luxor

Macedonia, Mars, Mazda, Mediterranean, Medusa, Memphis, Menelaus, Mercury, Midas, Minerva, moon, Muses, Myrtle

Narcissus, Neptune, Nero, Nike

Oceanus, Odin, Odysseus, Odyssey, Oedipus, Olympic, Olympus, Oracle, Orestes, Orion, owl

Palladium, Pallas, Palmyra, Pandora, Pantheon, Paris, Parthenon, Pegasus, Pella, Penelope, Pericles, Perseus, Phaedra, Phaeton, Pharos, Phoebe, Phoenix, Phoenicia, Phosphor, Phineus, Plato, Pluto, Pomona, Poseidon, Psyche, Pygmalion, pyramid

Ra, raven, Remus, Rhodes, Rome

Samson, Saturn, scorpion, Sibyl, Sirens, Sisyphus, Socrates, Sol, Sparta, Sphinx, Syracuse

Taliesin, Tempe, Thebes, Theseus, Thespian, Thor, Thracia, Titans, Tritan, Taliesin, Trojan, troll, Troy, Tutankamen, Tyre

Ulysses, Unicorn, Urania, Uranus, Ursa, Utica

Valhalla, Vega, Venus, Vesper, Vesta, vetta, Victoria, Viking, Virgil, Virgo, Vola, Vulcan

Xerxes

Zephyr, Zeus

III - 3
Universe and Zodiac

Altair, Amor, Andromeda (the chained lady), Antares, Aquarius (water carrier), Aquila (eagle), Archimedes, Arcturus, Aries (ram), Argus (starry sky), astro, astronomy, Auriga

Bellatrix, big bang, Big Dipper, binary, black hole, Borealis, Boreas (north wind)

Cancer (crab), Carina, Capricorn (horned goat), Capella, Cassiopeia (lady in the chair), Celestial, Centaurus (centaur), Cetus, Columba, comet, constellation, Corona Australis (southern crown), Corona Borealis (northern crown), Corvus, cosmic, cosmos, crescent, Cronos (time), Crux, Cygnus (swan)

Dawn, Delphinus (dolphin), Diomedes, Dione, Dionysus, Dorado

Earth, Eclipse, equinox, Europa, Eurus (east wind), Euripides

galactic, galaxy, Gemini (twins), globe

halo, Hercules, Hydra (water monster)

infrared, Io (moon)

Leo (lion), Libra (balance), light-year, Little Dipper, lunar, Lupus (wolf), Lynx, Lyra

Mensa (table mountain), meteor, Milky Way, moon

nebula, North Star, Notus (north wind), nova

orbit, Orion (the hunter)

parallax, Pegasus (winged horse), Phoenix, Pisces (fish), planet, (planets, see Ancient and Mythological list), Polaris, Pollux, Procyon, pulsar, Pyxis (mariner's compass)

Regulus

Sagitta (arrow), Sagittarius (archer), Scorpio (scorpion), Scorpius, sky, solar, solstice, Southern Cross, star, sun, Spica

Taurus (bull)

Ursa Major, Ursa Minor, unicorn

Vega, Vela (sails), Vesta (asteriod), Virgo (virgin)

Zephyrus (west wind), zenith, zodiac

III - 4
Famous People

Names included are generally those associated with leadership, creativity, discovery, or notoriety. There is an emphasis on American founding fathers, explorers, and frontier heros, as might be expected. Literary and biblical names, although having high recognition value, are downplayed as not being useful in a wide spectrum of naming situations. Name recognition, catchy nicknames, and incorporation into popular lore sometimes prevail over accomplishment.

Duplicate warning: Do not use the name of a living or recently deceased person (famous or not), or a United States president whose widow is living, in a business name without first obtaining written consent. Consult your lawyer. Such names are omitted from this list.

Abigail Adams, John Adams, Alexander the Great, Queen Anne, Susan B. Anthony, Aristotle, John Jacob Astor, John James Audubon, Stephen F. Austin

Johann Sebastian Bach, Vasco de Balboa, Phineas T. Barnum, Clara Barton, Ludwig van Beethoven, Alexander Graham Bell, Sarah Bernhardt, Black Hawk, William Blackstone, Humphrey Bogart, Anne Boleyn, William H. "Billy the Kid" Bonney, Daniel Boone, James Bowie, James B. "Diamond Jim" Brady, Johannes Brahms, Beau Brummell, Martha "Calamity Jane" Burke, Robert Burns

Antoine Cadillac, Galus Julius Caesar, John C. Calhoun, Al Capone, Christopher "Kit" Carson, George Washington Carver, Charles S. "Charlie" Chaplin, Agatha Christie, Winston L. S. Churchill, William Clark, Cleopatra, Ty Cobb, Cochise, William F. "Buffalo Bill" Cody, Christopher Columbus, Confucius, Captain James Cook, Copernicus, F. V. de Coronado, Crazy Horse, David "Davy" Crockett,

Marie "Madame" Curie, George Armstrong Custer

Clarence Darrow, Charles Darwin, Jefferson Davis, Jack Dempsey, Charles Dickens, Benjamin Disraeli, Frederick Douglass, Sir Francis Drake

Amelia Earhart, Wyatt Earp, Thomas Alva Edison, Albert Einstein, Eric the Red

Peter Carl Fabergé, Fanny Farmer, W. C. Fields, Benjamin Franklin, Galileo Galilei, Mohandas Gandhi, Greta Garbo, Genghis Khan, Geronimo, William Gladstone, Red Grange, Ulysses S. Grant, Zane Grey, Johann Gutenberg, Woody Guthrie

Nathan Hale, Alexander Hamilton, John Hancock, Edmund Halley, Hannibal, John Harvard, Nathaniel Hawthorne, Ernest Hemingway, Sonja Henie, Henry VIII, Alfred Hitchcock, James B. "Wild Bill" Hickok, Oliver Wendell Holmes, Homer, Sam Houston, Harry Houdini, Henry Hudson

Queen Isabella I

Andrew Jackson, Thomas J. "Stonewall" Jackson, Thomas Jefferson, Joan of Arc, Johnny Appleseed, John Paul Jones, Chief Joseph

King Kamehameha I, William "Captain" Kidd, Rudyard Kipling

Marquis de Lafayette, Lillie Langtry, R. D. LaSalle, Lawrence of Arabia, Robert E. Lee, Leonardo da Vinci, Meriwether Lewis, Queen Liliuokalani, Abraham Lincoln, Charles A. Lindbergh, John Griffith "Jack" London, Harry "Sundance Kid" Longabaugh, Henry Wadsworth Longfellow

Douglas MacArthur, Dolley Madison, James Madison, Ferdinand Magellan, Malcoln X, Horace Mann, Marie Antoinette, John Marshall, Groucho Marx, Mary Queen of Scots, Bat Masterson, Samuel A. Maverick, Michelangelo, Marilyn Monroe, Montezuma II, J. P. Morgan, Wolfgang Amadeus Mozart

Napoleon Bonaparte, Nefertiti, Horatio Nelson, Sir Isaac Newton, Florence Nightingale, Alfred B. Nobel, Nostradamus

Omar Kayyám

Robert L. "Butch Cassidy" Parker, George S. Patton, Oliver Hazzard Perry, John L. "Black Jack" Pershing, Zebulon M. Pike, Allan Pinkerton, Lydia Pinkham, Plato, Pocahontas, Edgar Allen Poe, Marco Polo, Madame de Pompadour, John Wesley Powell

Sir Walter Raleigh, Rameses II, Rasputin, Red Cloud, Red Jacket, Rembrandt van Ryn, Frederic Remington, Paul Revere, Richard the Lion-Hearted, Edward V. "Eddie" Rickenbacker, John D. Rockefeller, Knute Rockne, Norman Rockwell, William "Will" Rogers, Eleanor R., Franklin Delano, and Theodore "Teddy" Roosevelt, George Herman "Babe" Ruth

Sacajawea, Elizabeth "Nellie Bly" Seaman, William Shakespeare, George Bernard Shaw, William Tecumseh Sherman, Sitting Bull, Socrates, Harriet Beecher Stowe, Billy Sunday

Ida M. Tarbell, Zachary Taylor, Edward "Blackbeard" Teach, Tecumseh, William Tell, Jim Thorp, Tutankhamen, Mark Twain

George Vancouver, Cornelius Vanderbilt, Queen Victoria, Vincent van Gogh

George and Martha Washington, Daniel Webster, Arthur Wellesley Duke of Wellington, Mae West, Walt Whitman, Eli Whitney, Oscar Wilde, Frank Lloyd Wright, Orville and Wilbur Wright

III - 5
Americana

The names below are mostly place-names and nicknames, selected for their sight, sound, historical significance, and/or patriotic-emotional charge. Some probably should only be used in geographic context (Alamo, lone star), but others are all-purpose American words (Broadway, Columbia, Hollywood, New York), useable in many situations. Many, of course, are terribly overused. Native American names are perhaps overrepresented, but, even in translation, they are some of the most distinctively "American" words. Likewise "western" names.

A reminder: Continue to be alert for word parts to use in combination. For instance, I have always thought Ann Arbor, Michigan was an exceptionally beautiful place-name. Anne Arundel County, Maryland, is included for the same reason. Others that come to mind: Cape Cod, Massachusetts; Oyster Bay, New York; Glen Ellen, California. They exemplify the hundreds of distinctive local names around the country, far too many to include here. Using the Word Parts — Geographic list found in Chapter III-23, we could create Annfield, Glenanne, West Ann, etc.

Once you have found a name you like, be sure to search for earlier spellings that might lead you to a more distinctive trademark or trade name.

Abilene, Adirondack, Alaska, Alamo, Algonquin, Allegheny, Amarillo, America, America the Beautiful, American, Anchorage, Ann Arbor, Anne Arundel County, Annapolis, Antietam, Apache, Appalachian, Appomattox, Arizona, Arlington, Aspen, Astoria

Badlands, bald eagle, Beverly Hills, Big Apple, Big Bend, Big Sur, Blackfeet, Black Hills, bluegrass, Blue Ridge Mountains, Boardwalk, Boulder, Bowery, Brandywine, Broadway, Brooklyn, Bull

Run, Bunker Hill, Paul Bunyan

California, Calumet, Cape Cod, Cape Hatteras, Carolina, Cascade Range, Seventh Cavalry, Cayuse, Chapel Hill, Chattanooga, Lake Chelan, Cherokee, Chesapeake Bay, Chevy Chase, Cheyenne, Chicago, Chinook, Chippewa, Chisholm Trail, Cimarron, City of Angels, Clipper Ship, Colorado, Colt 45, Columbia River, Comanche, Concord Bridge, Coney Island, Constitution, Cooperstown, cowboy, Cripple Creek, Cumberland Gap

Dakota, Death Valley, Delaware, Deseret, Diamond Head, Dixie, Dodge City, Durango

Eagle, El Paso, Everglades

Flying Cloud, forty-niner, Fourth of July, frontier

Gettysburg, Glacier Bay, Golden Gate, Grand Canyon, Grand Forks, Great Smoky Mountains,

Harper's Ferry, Harvard, Haverhill, Hawaii, Hells Canyon, Hialeah, High Point, Hollywood, Honolulu, Hopi, Hudson River

Iroquois

Jackson Hole

Kachina, Kalamazoo, Kentucky, Key Largo, Key West, Kickapoo River, Kitty Hawk, Kodiak, Kokopelli

Laredo, Lexington, Liberty, Liberty Bell, Little America, Little Bighorn, Lodi, lone star, longhorn, Lost Dutchman, Louisiana

Malibu, Mandan, Manhattan, Martha's Vineyard, Mason-Dixon Line, Mayflower, Mendocino, Mesa, Mesquite, Minnehaha, Minuteman, Mississippi River, Missouri River, Mohawk, Mojave, Monterey, Monticello, Monument Valley, Mystic

Nantucket, Natchez Trace, Navajo, New Haven, New York, Niagara Falls, Northwest Passage

Oahu, OK Corral, Okefenokee, Oklahoma, Old Faithful, Old Ironsides, Old South, Oneida, Oregon Trail

Palo Alto, Palm Springs, Panhandle, Pasadena, Pearl Harbor, Pecos Bill, Pike's Peak, pioneer, Plymouth Rock, Princeton, Puritan

Range, rawhide, Red River, Red Wing, Roanoke, Rockies, Rocky Mountains, rodeo, Rogue River, Rough Rider, Mt. Rushmore

Sacramento, Saginaw Bay, St. Augustine, Salishan, San Francisco, San Juan Hill, Santa Catalina Island, Santa Fe Trail, Saratoga Springs, Seneca, Mt. Shasta, Shawnee, Shenandoah, Shilo, Shoshone, Sierra Nevada, Sioux, Spirit of St. Louis, Stars and Stripes Forever, Star Spangled Banner, Sunnyvale

Lake Tahoe, Taos, Tar Heel, Teapot Dome, Tecumseh, tepee, Texas, Thousand Oaks, Ticonderoga, Tippecanoe, Tombstone, Tucson

Uncle Sam

Valley Forge, Mt. Vernon, Virginia

Wagon train, Waikiki, Walden Pond, Walla Walla, Washington, Wellesley, westward ho, West Point, Williamsburg, Winchester rifle, Wind River Range, Wyoming

Yankee, Yellowstone, Yosemite Valley

III - 6
Exotic Names from Around the World

Acadia, Acapulco, Aegean Sea, Africa, Algiers, Almadén, Amazon, Andes Mountains, Mt. Annapurna, Antarctica, Aquitania, Aragon, Arctic Circle, Athens, Azores Islands

Baghdad, Bahama Islands, Baja California, Bali, Banff, Barbary Coast, Bengal, Bermuda, Bohemia, Ciudad Bolivar, Bombay, Bonanza Creek, Bora Bora, Bordeaux, Borneo, Botany Bay, Burgundy, Burma

Cairo, Calcutta, Canary Islands, Cannes, Cape Horn, Capri, Casablanca, Cashmere, Castile, Congo, Coral Sea, Constantinople, Corinth, Cyprus

Damascus, Danube, Dawson Creek, Devil's Island

Easter Island, Egypt, equator, Ethiopia, Eurasia, Mt. Everest

Fez, Fiji, Fontainebleau, Forbidden City, Mt. Fuji

Galapagos Islands, Geneva, Gibraltar, Ginza, Gold Coast, Cape of Good Hope, Gran Chaco, Gran Paradiso, Great Barrier Reef, Grenada, Grenoble, Guadalupe, Gulf Stream

Havana, Hawaii, Himalaya Mountains, Hindu Kush Mountains, Hispaniola, Hong Kong

Iberia, Imperia, Inca, Interlaken, Istanbul

Java, Jamaica

Kalahari Desert, Kashmir, Katmandu, Kenya, Khartoum, Khyber

Pass, Mt. Kilimanjaro, Kimberley, the Klondike, Komodo Island, Mount Kongur, Kuala Lumpur

Gulf of Laconia, La Paz, Lapland, Latin Quarter, Le Mans, Limpopo River, Lodi, Lombardy, Lucerne

Mackenzie River, Madagascar, Madiera, Madras, Malay, Malta, Strait of Magellan, Mandalay, Marrakesh, Marseilles, Martinique, Matterhorn, Maui, Mecca, Mediterranean Sea, Mexico, Monte Carlo, Mosquito Coast, Mozambique, Mykonos Island

Nassau, Naxos, Nepal, Nice, Nile River, North Pole, Novara

Odessa, Orleans

Pacific, Pago Pago, Palatine, Paris, Patagonia, Persia, Port Moresby, Pyrenees Mountains

Quebec

Rangoon, Rio de Janeiro, Rio Grande, Riviera, Rome, Rosario, Rosetta

Sahara Desert, Saint Helena Island, Samothrace, Scandinavia, Segovia, Serengeti Plain, Sevilla, Shanghai, Shangri-la, Siam, Siberia, Sierra Madre, Singapore, Snowy River, South Seas, Spice Islands, Suez

Tahiti, Tampico, Tangier, Taxco, Tasmania, Taxco, Tempe, Thunder Bay, Tibet, Tiburon, Tierra del Fuego, Tigris River, Timbuktu, Lake Titicaca, Tivoli, Trafalgar, Trieste, Tripoli, Tyrol

Valdivia, Valencia, Valparaiso, Venice, Veracruz, Cape Verde, Verona, Vesuvius, Lake Victoria, Vienna, Vladivostok, Volga River

Waterloo, Westphalia, Winterthur

Yangtze River, Yukon

Zanzibar, Zurich

III - 7
Beautiful Names from the British Isles

You see them everywhere in the United States and Canada, names imported from the "Mother Country." Some have become so familiar, fit so well, we hardly think of them as borrowed—Boston, Plymouth, Portland. Others cause an occasional raised eyebrow when naming luxury apartment buildings or tony subdivisions to make them appear exclusive—slightly artificial, but believable. Whatever. Although North America has place-names from many countries, British names seem to be in the majority, loaded with emotion and meaning—stability, snootiness, and hand-me-down nobility.

The following British place-names were taken from the *Times Atlas of the World*. I list the more popular names to save you the trouble. If not, use it as a base, and go at it yourself. You will be joining thousands of people before you, who peered at maps and directories of England, Scotland, and Ireland deep into the night, trying to find just the right name for their new street, subdivision, snazzy hotel, or whatever. Or their cigarette, such as Marlboro, from Marlborough.

Test carefully for ease of pronunciation before adoption. If you hesitate, as I do with Edinburgh, Scotland, forget it. You might also skip the shire-ending names, such as Nottinghamshire, as generally having one more syllable than Yanks can handle.

These words offer splendid opportunities for combining. Break them into their parts. Drop endings you do not care for. Create your own "British" name. That is how many were created in the first place. Again, see Chapter III-23, "Word Parts—Geographic."

Another point: Seek out or create names with associations conveying something more—more, that is, than snuggling up to ersatz dignity. For instance, Wellington brings to mind the duke of Wellington, who beat Napoleon at.... Brighton, Winchester, Newport, Winsford, and Highland all begin with positive-sounding word parts. The city of Stirling, Scotland, brings sterling, the monetary unit, to mind.

Abbot, Abby Wood, Aberdeen, Andover, Annan, Ardee, Argyle, Ascot, Ashbourne, Ashford, Avalon, Avon

Banbury, Bangor, Bedford, Belfast, Belford, Belvedre, Birmingham, Blackburn, Blarney, Blenham, Blyth, Bradford, Braemar, Brentwood, Bridgewater, Brighton, Bristol, Boston, Buckingham

Caledonia, Cambridge, Callander, Canterbury, Cardigan, Carrick, Carlisle, Chatham, Chelsea, Cheshire, Chester, Chesterfield, Chesterford, Chevoit Hills, Colwyn Bay, Coventry, Culloden Moor

Dartmouth, Derby, Derry, Devon, Doncaster, Donegal, Dorchester, Dorset, Douglas, Dover, Dublin, Dumbarton, Dunbar, Dundee, Dungeness, Durham

Edinburgh, Elgin, England, Epping Forest, Epsom, Erie, Essex, Eton, Exeter

Fair Isle, Faversham, Fleetwood

Gainsborough, Galloway, Galway, Glengarry, Gloucester, Great Glen of Scotland, Greenwich

Hackney, Halifax, Hampshire, Hampstead, Hampton, Harrow on the Hill, Hastings, Haverford, Henley-on-Thames, Highland, Holywood, Huntley, Hyde Park

Inverness, Ipswich, Ireland, Irvine

Jersey

Kells, Kensington, Kent, Kew, Kildare, Killarney, Kingsgate, Kingston, Kircaldy

Lancaster, Lancashire, Land's End, Limerick, Lincoln, Liverpool, London, Londonderry, Lyme Regis, Lymington

Manchester, Mansfield, Marlborough, Marylebone, Mayfair, Melrose,

Middleton, Montrose

Newcastle, Newport, Norfolk, Northhampton, Northwood, Nottingham

Oldham, Oxford

Paisley, Park Royal, Pembroke, Penzance, Pickering, Plymouth, Portland, Portsmouth, Prestwick

Ramsgate, Richmond, Rochdale, Rugby, Runnymede

St. Andrews, St. Albans, Sandhurst, Sandwich, Scarborough, Scone, Scotia, Scotland, Sedgemoor, Severn, Shannon, Sheffield, Sherwood, Shetland, Shrewsbury, Shropshire, Isle of Skye, Somerset, South Downs, Southgate, Southhampton, Squires Gate, Stafford, Stewart, Stirling, Stonehenge, Stonybridge, Stratford on Avon, Surry, Sussex

Tara, Taunton, River Tay, Tewkesbury, Thames, Thurrock, Tilbury, Tipperary, Tiverton, Torrington, Torquay, Tottenham, Tralee, Tweed, Twickenham, River Tyne

Valentia Island

Wakefield, Walden, Wales, Walford, Wallington, Warrington, Warwick, Waterford, Wellington, Wembley, Westchester, West End, Westminister, Weybourne, Weybridge, Whitby, Wimbledon, Wilmington, Windsor, Whitechapel, Whitehaven, Whitestone, Whittlesey, Wickham, Wiltshire, Winchester, Winsford, Windermere, Windsor, Woodstock, Worcester

York

III - 8
Prestige and Title Words

Admiral, admiralty, ambassador, aristocrat

Captain, castle, chairman of the board, chief, colonel, commander, commodore, congress, court, crown

Dame, diadem, director, distinguished, duke, duchess

Earl, elite, eminence, empire, esteem, exclusive

General, gentleman, grand

Highness, house of lords

Imperial

King, kingdom, knight

Lady, lieutenant, lord

Marquis, majestic, majesty, major, medal, medallion, monarch

Noble

Patrician, president, prestige, prince, princess

Queen

Regal, regent, regency, royal

Savoir-faire, scepter, senator, sir, sovereign

Throne, treasurer

VIP, vanguard, vice president, viscount

III - 9
Superlatives - Laudatory, Power, and Action Words

Remember, think word parts as well as words.

A-1, able, absolute, accelerated, acclaim, accomplish, accurate, acme, action, active, add, adept, advanced, advantage, adventure, alert, alive, all, alta, amazing, authentic, avalanche, awesome

Beneficial, beneficent, best, big, biggest, blue ribbon, bold, bonus, boss, brave, bright, brisk

Capital, celebrated, certain, certified, champion, chief, choice, class, colossal, colossus, competent, control, correct, courageous, create, creative, critical, current

Dare, daring, dawn, deluxe, dependable, design, direct, distinguished, double, durable, dynamic, dynamite

Early, edge, efficient, electric, electrify, elevate, energy, energetic, eureka, exact, exalted, excel, excellent, excelsior, excite, exciting, exemplary, exceptional, expert, express, extra

Fabulous, famous, fascinating, fast, favor, favorable, fierce, fine, first, first class, first rate, flash, fleet, flex, force, formidable, free, freedom, fresh, furious

Gain, genesis, genuine, giant, gigantic, global, glorious, glory, gold, golden, gold medal, good, grand, great, guard, guardian, guide

Head, high, honor, huge

Immediate, incredible, influential, initial, instant, integrity, intelligent, intense, invincible

Jiffy, joy, jumbo

Landmark, large, latest, leading, legendary, legitimate, lightning, lively, lofty

Mach, macro, magic, magnificent, magnum, majestic, mammoth, marathon, marvel, marvelous, massive, master, matchless, maximum, mega, might, mighty, miracle, modern, more, motion, multi, multiple

New, novel, now

Okay, one, optima, optimal, optimum, opulent, oracle, original, outstanding

Peak, peerless, pep, perfect, perfection, performance, phenomenon, pinnacle, pioneer, plus, positive, power, practical, precise, precision, preeminent, premier, premium, prestige, pride, primary, prime, prima, principle, pro, prodigy, professional, proficient, progressive, propitious, pure

Quality, quantum, quick

Rapid, reliable, remarkable, resolute, right, rise

Safe, salute, salutary, select, sensation, sensational, seize, sharp, singular, skill, smart, snap, snappy, soar, sonic, spark, sparkle, special, spectacular, speed, speedy, splendid, sterling, strategic, streak, strong, stunner, success, summit, super, superb, superior, superlative, supreme, swift

Tall, terrific, thrive, thriving, titan, titanic, today, top, top-notch, tough, tower, treasure, trend, triumph, true, turbo

Ultra, unique, unsurpassed, up, upper

Valor, value, vibrant, victor, vigor, virtue, vision, vivid

Whale, wisdom, wise, wonder, worth

Young

Zenith, zoom

III - 10
Emotion

Adorable, adore, adoration, affordable, allure, alluring, amiable, appeal, appealing, arouse, assist, attractive

Bargain, beautiful, benefit, bright, budget

Calm, care, carefree, cheer, chic, class, classy, clean, comfort, comfortable, console, content, convenient, cozy, cuddly

Debonair, delight, delightful, devotion, discount, discover, durable

Ease, easy, economy, economical, elegant, emotive, enchanting, exciting, exhilaration, exquisite

Feel, feeling, fond, fortune, free, fresh, friend, friendly, fulfillment

Gentle, glamorous, good, gorgeous, gracious, gratify

Handsome, handy, happy, heart, horizon, hug

In, independent, inspire, intimate, irresistible

Jubilant, joy, jolly

Kindness, kiss

Liberated, light, love, lovely, loving, lucky, lusty, luxurious, luxury

Mellow, memorable, memory, merry, mythical

Natural

Passion, passionate, peace, peaceful, pleasant, please, pleasure, pledge, plush, praise, pretty

Quiet

Rare, ready, refined, refresh, refreshing, relax, relief, rest, rich, romantic, rugged

Safe, satisfy, secure, security, sensitive, sensual, sensuous, serene, slender, slim, smile, snug, soft, solace, sooth, spirit, spring, sturdy, success, sweet

Tantalizing, tender, thrill, thrilling, tidy, timely, touch, touched, tranquil, trim, trust, trustworthy

Warm, warmth, wealth, wonder, wonderful

Zest

III - 11
The Natural World

From the Chicago Bears to the Pony Express, we have always named things after the animals and birds—fish, insects, and reptiles, too. They fall into a pattern, of course. We select hunters over the hunted, carnivorous over grazing animals, more or less solitary animals over herding types. Seldom do we see companies, products, or services named after eels, goldfish, lambs, snakes, pigeons, shrimp, minnows, weasels, and the like.

Since the lists in Part III are supposed to save you the time and effort of pulling all this together, my plan was to edit out the shrimp and minnows, which you would never, *never* use for business names. These lists are supposed to be selective, realistic, and right to the point. On reflection, however, maybe there are offbeat companies and products that are appropriate Shrimp and Minnows. Perhaps I was being too judgmental. Who would ever have imagined the meaning now attached to the names Batman and Robin. Think about it. So, "pop goes the weasel," back onto the list.

More popular than one might think are names from the plant world, flowers and trees. They name everything you can think of, from computer programs to automobiles (Lotus), to restaurants (Jasmine Garden, Evergreen Cafe), to boutiques (Gilded Orchid, Poppy Seed Emporium).

If you have a favorite living thing you would like to incorporate into a name, be sure to look in the dictionary to check secondary meanings and find Latin variations with potential. For example, peregrine falcon. Peregrine means wandering, migratory, a pilgrim. The Latin word for falcon is *Falco*, which is not a bad-sounding business name by itself. Lion is *Panthera leo*; tiger, *Panthera tigris;* etc. I like the name for the timber rattlesnake, *Crotalus horridus*. Don't laugh. There are hundreds of *horridus* products out there.

III - 12
Mammals

Aardvark, addax, alpaca, anteater, antelope, ape, armadillo

Badger, bat, bear, beaver, bighorn, bison, bobcat, bronco, buffalo, bull, bulldog, buck, burro

Camel, canine, cat, chameleon, chamois, cheetah, chimpanzee, chinchilla, cougar, coyote

Deer, dog

Eland, elephant, elk, ermine

Ferret, fox

Giraffe, goat, gopher, gorilla, grizzly bear, guinea pig

Hare, hedgehog, hippopotamus, hog, horse, hyena, hyrax

Ibex, impala

Jackal, jackrabbit, jaguar

Kinkajou, koala

Leopard, lion, llama, lynx

Mammoth, marten, mink, mole, mongoose, moose, mountain goat, mouse, musk ox

Ocelot, otter, ox

Pachyderm, panda, panther, peccary, pig, pika, polar bear, polecat, pony, prairie dog, puma

Rabbit, raccoon, ram, raptor, rat, razorback, reindeer, rhinoceros

Sable, serval, sheep, shrew, skunk, sloth

Timber wolf, tiger

Vicuña

Warthog, water buffalo, weasel, wildebeest, wolf, wolverine

Zebra

II - 13
Fish and Sea Creatures

Albacore, alewife, anchovy, angelfish

Barnacle, barracuda, bass, bluefin tuna, bonito, bullhead

Carp, catfish, char, chinook salmon, chub, chum salmon, clam, codfish, coho salmon, coral, crab, cuttlefish

Darter, dolphin, dorado

Eel

Flounder, flying fish

Gar, goldfish, grouper, grunion, guppy

Haddock, hake, halibut, hatchet fish, herring

Jellyfish

Killer whale, krill

Lamprey, lingcod, lobster

Mackerel, man-of-war, manatee, manta ray, marlin, menhaden, mermaid, mussel, muskellunge

Nautilus, nepa

Perch, periwinkle, pickerel, pike, pilotfish, piranha, pompano, porpoise

Octopus, orca, oyster

Ray, remora

Sailfish, salmon, sardine, scallop, sculpin, seahorse, seal, sea lion, shad, shark, shell, shrimp, snapper, sockeye salmon, squid, starfish, sturgeon, sucker, swordfish

Tarpon, tortoise, trout, tuna, turtle

Walrus, whale, whiting, walleye

III - 14
Reptiles

Alligator

Boa constrictor, box turtle, bushmaster snake

Chameleon, coachwhip snake, cobra, copperhead, coral snake, cottonmouth moccasin, crocodile

Desert tortoise, diamondback rattler, dinosaur, dragon lizard

Eyelash viper

Galapagos tortoise, garter snake, gecko, green turtle

Horned lizard

Iguana, indigo snake

King cobra, komodo lizard, leatherback sea turtle

Lizard

Monitor lizard, mud turtle

Pit viper, pterodactyl, puff adder, pygmy rattlesnake, python

Rattlesnake

Scarlet king snake, sea turtle, sidewinder, snake, snapping turtle

Terrapin, tortoise, turtle

Viper

III - 15
Insects

Ambrosia beetle, ant, aphid, army ant, assassin bug, atlas moth

Bedbug, bee, bumblebee, beetle, black fly, blowfly, bug, butterfly

Caddisfly, carpenter ant, caterpillar, cecropia moth, chigger, cicada, cockroach, cocoon, cricket

Daddy longlegs, damselfly, desert locust, digger wasp, dragonfly

Earwig

Fairyfly, flea, firefly, flea beetle, formica ant, fruit fly, furniture beetle

Gnat, gold bug, grasshopper, grub

Harlequin cabbage bug, harvester ant, honeybee, horsefly, housefly, hornet

Inchworm, io moth

Janitor ant, june beetle

Katydid

Lacewing, ladybug, locust, louse, luna moth

Maggot, mantis, mayfly, metamorphosis, midge, millepede, monarch butterfly, mosquito, moth, mud-dauber wasp

Nymph

Painted lady butterfly, paper wasp, phantom crane fly, pine sphinx, praying mantis

Queen bee

Roach

Sand flea, sawfly, scorpion, silkworm moth, silverfish, Spanish fly, spider, sphinx moth, stinkbug, stonefly

Termite, thrip, tick, tiger beetle, tsetse fly

Velvet ant, vinegar fly

Walking-stick, wasp, water beetle, water boatman, water bug, water strider, weevil, whirligig beetle

Yellowjacket, yucca moth

III - 16
Birds

Albatross, auk, avocet

Bald eagle, barn owl, bat, bird of paradise, bittern, blackbird, blue jay, bobwhite, booby, bullfinch, bunting

Canary, cardinal, chickadee, chicken, condor, coot, cormorant, crane, crow, cuckoo, curlew

Dove, dodo, duck

Eagle, egret, eider duck, emperor penguin, emu

Falcon, finch, fish hawk, flamingo, flycatcher

Gannet, golden eagle, goldfinch, goose, great horned owl, gull

Hawk, heron, hummingbird

Ibis

Jay, junco

Kingfisher, kite, kiwi, kookaburra

Lark, loon, lovebird

Magpie, mallard duck, marabou, merganser, mockingbird, murre, myna bird

Nighthawk, nutcracker

Oriole, osprey, ostrich, owl

Parrot, partridge, pelican, penguin, peregrine falcon, petrel, pigeon, pintail duck, plover, puffin

Quetzal

Raven, roadrunner, robin

Sandpiper, scarlet tanager, screech owl, shrike, skimmer, snipe, snow goose, sparrow, sparrow hawk, spoonbill, starling, stork, swallow, swan

Tern, thrush, titmouse, tomtit, toucan, towhee, turkey

Vesper sparrow, vireo, vulture

Warbler, waxwing, whippoorwill, woodcock, woodpecker

Yellowlegs

III - 17
Trees

Alder, ash, aspen

Balsam, bamboo, beech, birch, buckeye

Cedar, catalpa, chaparral, cherry, chestnut, cinnamon, conifer, cottonwood, crab apple, cypress

Dogwood

Elm, eucalyptus

Fig, fir

Ginkgo, guava

Hawthorn, hazel, hibiscus, hickory, holly

Jacaranda, jujube, juniper

Kumquat

Larch, lignum vitae

Magnolia, mahogany, manzanita, maple, mesquite, mulberry, myrrh, myrtle

Oak, olive, orange

Palm, pawpaw, pear, persimmon, piñon pine, plum, poplar

Rosewood

Sandalwood, sassafras, spruce, sumac, sycamore

Tupelo

Viburnum

Wahoo, walnut, willow, witch hazel

Yew

III - 18
Plants

Absinthe, acacia, alfalfa, almond, aloe, amaryllis, angelica, anise, apple, apricot, arrowroot, artichoke, aspic, aster, azalea

Baby's breath, bachelor's button, banana, barley, basil, bean, beet, belladonna, bird of paradise, black-eyed Susan, bleeding heart, bluebell, blueberry, bluebonnet, bougainvillea, broccoli, Brussels sprouts, bullrush, buttercup

Cabbage, cactus, calabash, calla lily, calyx, camellia, caraway, cardamon, carnation, carrot, catnip, cattail, cauliflower, chamomile, cherry, chickweed, chicory, chive, chrysanthemum, clematis, clove, clover, cockscomb, collard, columbine, coriander, cornflower, corolla, corona, cotton, cowslip, cranberry, crocus, cumin, currant

Daffodil, dahlia, daisy, dandelion, delphinium, dill

Edelweiss

Flax, forget-me-not, forsythia, foxglove, fuchsia

Gardenia, garland, geranium, ginger, ginseng, gloxinia, goldenrod, gooseberry, gorse

Heather, heliotrope, herb, herbal, hibiscus, hollyhock, honeysuckle, horseradish, hyacinth, hydrangea, hyssop

Indian pipe, indigo, iris, ivy

Jack-in-the-pulpit, Jacob's ladder, jambalaya, jasmine, jimsonweed, jonquil

Kava, kohlrabi, kudzu

Lady's slipper, lavender, licorice, lilac, lily, lily of the valley, lime, lotus, lupine

Marigold, marjoram, milkweed, mint, morning glory

Narcissus, nasturtium, nettle, nutmeg

Okra, oleander, onion, orchid, oregano

Pansy, parsley, pea, peach, peanut, pear, peony, peppermint, periwinkle, petunia, phlox, pimpernel, poison ivy, poplar, poppy, posy, potpourri, prickly pear, primrose

Quince

Radish, ragweed, rhododendron, rose, rosemary, royal poinciana

Safflower, saffron, sage, sarsparilla, savory, saxifrage, senna, shooting star, shamrock, skunk cabbage, snapdragon, snowdrop, spearmint, spinach, spirea, squash, strawberry, string bean, sunflower, sweet pea, sweet potato, sweet William, sweetbrier, sycamore

Tarragon, thistle, thyme, tiger lily, tulip, turnip

Vermouth, vetch, violet

Water lily, willow, wintergreen, wisteria, woodruff

Yarrow, yucca

Zinnia

III - 19
Colors

Alabaster, almond, amber, apricot, aqua, aquamarine, auburn, avocado

Beige, black, blond, blue, brindle, bronze, brown, buff, burgundy

Canary, caramel, cardinal, carmine, cerise, cerulean, champagne, charcoal, chartreuse, cherry, chestnut, chocolate, cinnabar, cinnamon, citron, claret, cobalt blue, cochineal, cocoa, coffee, copper, coral, cream, crimson, crocus, cyan

Daffodil, dandelion, dun

Ebony, ecru, eggshell, emerald

Faience, fawn, flamingo, flax, fuchsia

Garnet, geranium, ginger, gold, grape, gray, green, gunmetal

Hazel, heather, heliotrope, henna, hyacinth

Indigo, ivory

Jasmine

Khaki

Lavender, lemon, lilac, liver

Magenta, mahogany, maize, maroon, mauve, mocha, molasses, mulberry, mustard

Nasturtium, navy blue, nutmeg

Oak, ocher, olive, onyx, orange, orchid, oxblood

Pansy, paprika, peach, pearl, petunia, pink, platinum, plum, poppy, pumpkin, purple, putty

Raspberry, red, rose, royal blue, ruby, russet, rust

Sable, saffron, salmon, sand, sanguine, sapphire, scarlet, sepia, sienna, silver, slate, smoke, sorrel, steel, straw, sunflower

Tan, tangerine, taupe, teak, turquoise

Ultramarine, umber

Vermeil, vermillion, violet

White, wine

Yellow

III - 20
Financial

Advance, affluent, afford, affordable, annuity

Bank, benefactor, beneficial, benefit, bond, bottom line, buck

Capital, capitalize, cash, coin, coffer, coin, commercial, consortium, credit, currency

Deposit, dime, dividend, dollar

Eagle, economics, economy, escrow, exchequer

Fiduciary, finance, fiscal, fortune, fund, funding

Gold, gold standard, greenback

Income, increase, interest, invest, investment

Layaway, legacy, leverage, loan

Million, millionaire, mint, money, monetary, moneyed, multi, multiply, mutual fund

Nest egg, nickel

Pecuniary, penny, penny-wise, pension, pin money, platinum, pocketbook, pound, premium, principal, profit, progress, promise, promissory note, purse, pyramid

Remit, remittance, reserve, return, revenue, reward, rise

Safe, safety, save, saving, Scotch, secure, security, shelter, silver, specie, standard, sum

Talent, tax shelter, treasure, treasurer, treasury

Up, upswing

Value, valuable, venture, venture capital, vest

Wallet, wampum, war chest, wealth, well heeled

Yield

III - 21
All-Purpose Phrases

Do you remember the TV program "Moonlighting," with Bruce Willis and Cybil Shepherd? The fictional company they worked for was the Blue Moon Detective Agency. The name comes from the phrase/idiom/cliché "once in a blue moon." It has wide recognition value, just the thing for naming, even if we do not know exactly what a blue moon is. How many Blue Moon bookstores, gift shops, cafes, taverns, etc., exist around the country we can only guess.

Following is a list of phrases, many of which have been used as business names at one time or another. Your town may not be dying for another Blue Moon Cafe, but Blue Moon Process Servers may be just right. The phrases are not classified for use by any particular business; it is up to you to make the fit. Some have been shortened to begin with the most recognizable word. Most of the many phrases of a negative nature were omitted, being inappropriate for the vast majority of naming opportunities. For example: scraping the bottom of the barrel, fly the coop, bull in a china shop.

Since names of this sort are often of a whimsical nature, precision is of little concern. Simple recognition of the phrase in the subject's context may be enough. For instance, calling an eatery Too Many Cooks, as in "too many cooks spoil the broth," might have the desired jocular effect. The audience has the pleasure of filling in the rest of the phrase/cliché (thus, not only gaining their attention with a catchy name, but enticing them to linger a moment, reinforcing their memories), knows immediately that it is tongue-in-cheek humor, and that it is most likely a restaurant.

Again, the "farther out" of expected context the phrase is used, the more distinctive (sometimes) it becomes. One of my droll favorites, Poor Taste, names a funky clothing store in San Francisco. At the extreme are phrases overused to the point where they become trite—clichés. The more sophisticated the audience, the more "turned off" they may be by them—the risk factor. A different audience, however, may receive a positive message. Crude clichés may be "just the ticket." (See how easy it is to lapse into cliché usage.) The point is to pay careful attention to the desired effect, and to know the target customer/audience as thoroughly as possible.

I cannot resist quoting three of my most hated clichés in the desperate hope that you will never use them in naming: "light as a feather," "totally new concept," and "world's greatest...."

The list:

A to Z, above and beyond, according to Hoyle, ace in the hole, Aesop's fables, against the grain, all of your marbles, all over town, all talk, all that glitters is not gold, all the way, all work and no play, all the aces, apple of my eye, apple pie order, apron strings, armed to the teeth, as good as done, asleep at the switch, at ease, ax to grind

Back in circulation, bag and baggage, bag of tricks, ball rolling, beauty is only skin deep, beck and call, Bermuda Triangle, best foot forward, best of everything, best shot, best wishes, better days, bird in the hand, black sheep, blow your mind, body and soul, bolt out of the blue, both feet, bound for glory, break away, break the ice, breath of fresh air, bright and early, bright idea, bull's-eye, bursting with pride, busy beaver, by heart, by the dozen, by the numbers, by the skin of your teeth

Carried away, cash-and-carry, cat and mouse, catch your breath, cat out of the bag, cheer up, China gate, clean sweep, clear blue sky, close shave, cloud nine, coast-to-coast, cock-and-bull, cold turkey, coming and going, coming of age, crazy quilt, credit is due, cross a bridge, cross my heart, cutting edge, cum laude

Davy Jones's locker, dead to rights, deep end, different drummer, down to earth, dream come true, dressed to kill, driving force, duck soup, ducks in a row

Eagle's nest, ear to the ground, easy street, eat your heart out, edge on someone, eyeteeth

Fair weather, fair shake, familiar ring, far and wide, fast buck, finger in the pie, feel like a million, fish to fry, flying colors, foot in the door, for keeps, free reign, French connection, from the bottom up, full swing

Garden path, get the show on the road, get up and go, get wind of it, gift horse, gift of gab, give it the gun, give me a break, glad hand, go-ahead, go bananas, go fly a kite, go for broke, going places, gold digger, Golden Fleece, golden rule, gold mine, good account, good as gold, good faith, goose bumps, go to town, Grand Prix, grand slam, grease monkey, great balls of fire, great guns, Great Wall of China, green light, green thumb, green with envy, grin and bear it, grist for the mill, Gulliver's travels, guys and dolls

Half a loaf, hammer and tongs, hand in hand, hand-me-down, hand over fist, hang tough, hard-and-fast, hard as nails, hard sell, hard up, hat in the ring, have your cake, head and shoulders, head start, heart and soul, heart of gold, heart's content, heart stand still, heart-to-heart, heave-ho, heaven and earth, high and mighty, high gear, high on the hog, high sign, high time, hit the jackpot, hit the spot, hog wild, holding the bag, hold a candle, home fires burning, hot seat, house and home

In a jiffy, in a nutshell, in a word, in cahoots, in clover, industrial strength, in from the cold, in one ear and out the other, in love, in line, in shape, inside out, inside track, in the bag, in the cards, in the chips, in the groove, in the limelight, in the money, in the mood, into orbit, irons in the fire, it figures, it's a deal, ivory tower

Just desserts, just for kicks, jump the gun

Kettle of fish, kick up your heels, kid gloves, know the ropes

Lame duck, land on your feet, last laugh, last resort, last word, lay it on the line, lead off, leaps and bounds, leave well enough alone, lend an ear, lend a hand, let your hair down, liberty bell, license to kill, lick and a promise, life of Riley, light at the end of the tunnel, light of day, like a house afire, like clockwork, line of duty, live it up, lock, stock, and barrel, long run, long shot, looking forward to something, looking good, look like a million dollars, love at first sight, love nor money

Mad as a hatter, make a name for yourself, make good money, make hay while the sun shines, make yourself at home, make waves, March hare, measure up, merry chase, middle of nowhere, mind your own business, mind your p's and q's, money talks, money to burn, monkey business, month of Sundays, Murphy's law

Name dropping, name of the game, needle in a haystack, never had it so good, Newton's apple, nick of time, night and day, nine-to-five, nip and tuck, nose to the grindstone, no stone unturned, now and again, nose in a book, nuts about you

Off the hook, of the first water, old shoe, old stamping ground, once-over, on a roll, on target, on the ball, on the double, on the horizon, on the loose, on the Q.T., on the spot, on the wing, on top of the world, on the line, once in a blue moon, once-in-a-lifetime, one good turn deserves another, one of these days, only have eyes for you, out of the corner of my eye, out of this world, over a barrel, over the top, over your head

Paint the town red, pat on the back, pay dirt, penny saved, pick-me-up, pins and needles, plain English, play fair, playing with fire, poor little lambs, pretty penny, pretty pickle, purse strings, put something by

Quick on the draw, quick as a wink

Rags to riches, rain or shine, read between the lines, red ball, red carpet, red cent, right arm, right mind, right up your alley, ring a bell, rock and a hard place, rock and roll, rocks in your head, rolling stone, roll out the red carpet, rose garden, rubbing elbows, run for your money, running start

Save the day, scratch my back, screw loose, second childhood, second thoughts, second wind, see daylight, set your sights, set the world on fire, seventh heaven, sewed up, shape up, short order, short work, silk purse, silver dollar, sitting duck, sitting pretty, skin of your teeth, sky high, snug as a bug in a rug, something coming, song and dance, south sea, spade a spade, square accounts, stars in your eyes, strike up the band, sweet tooth

Take the cake, talk of the town, teacher's pet, taut ship, that's the way the cookie crumbles, the early bird gets the worm, the long haul, the works, thick and thin, third degree, Three Musketeers, three ring circus, tie the knot, to and fro, ton of bricks, tortoise and hare, too many cooks spoil the broth, too much of a good thing, toss your hat in the ring, to the ends of the earth, tough nut to crack, tricks of the trade, trump card, turn for the better, turn over a new leaf, twinkling of an eye, two cents' worth

Under your hat, up-and-coming, up and up, up front, up to date, use every trick in the book

Vanish into thin air

Walking papers, wear more than one hat, well heeled, well-to-do, what's cooking?, what's up?, when the cat's away the mice will play, where there's a will there's a way, whole nine yards, word for word, worth its weight in gold, wrong side of the bed

X marks the spot

Yes sir, that's my baby, you can't tell a book by its cover, your cup of tea, yours truly

Zoom in

III - 22
Sports Terms

Because of their instant recognition, sports terms provide many opportunities for business names, especially products and services. Remember, however, names and nicknames of actual teams, as well as other names and terms, may be registered trademarks—Super Bowl, Razorbacks, Little League, Windsurfer, etc.

Ace, across the board, airball, all-American, all-star

Babe Ruth, back flip, ball four, base camp, bases loaded, batter up, because it is there, biathlon, birdie, Black Sox, bogey, box score, break the tape

Carry the ball, century, cheerleader, chip shot, class five, country club, cross-country, crown, cup, crying towel, curveball

Decathlon, derby, discus, divot, double-header, down the stretch, duffer, dunk

Eagle, eye on the ball

Face-off, fair catch, fairway, false start, fastball, field of dreams, finish line, first ascent, first base, first down, first string, fly ball, forecourt, four-minute mile, foursome, franchise, freestyle, fullback

Gladiator, goal, goal line stand, go for the gold, grand slam, gridiron

Half nelson, halftime, hall of fame, harrier, hash mark, hat trick, heavyweight, Heidi game, hole in one, homestretch, home run

Immaculate Reception, inside track, intercept, in the hole, in the paint

Javelin, jock, jockey, jog, judo

Kayo, kickoff, kingpin, knockout punch, Kung Fu

Left field, lineup, love

Magic, major leagues, man-to-man, marathon, medalist, minor league, Mr. Touchdown, motocross, mountaineer

No hitter, nothing but net, number one

Off base, off sides, on deck, overtime

Paddock, par, penalty box, pigskin, pinch-hit, play ball, playoff, point a minute, Pride of the Yankees, psyched out, put him away

Raging Bull, rebound, rain check, red shirt, road game, road work, roll out, rookie, Rugby, run for the roses

Sacrifice fly, seventh-inning stretch, shortstop, shot clock, shutout, sky dive, slalom, slam dunk, spike the ball, split the uprights, sprint, stadium, steel curtain, strikeout, strike three, suck it up, superstar, surfboard, swish

T-formation, take me out to the ballgame, the Babe, the Bums, three yards and a cloud of dust, top ten, to the showers, trash talk, traverse, triathlon, triple axel, triple double, turnover, two platoon

Underdog, uppercut, upper deck

Varsity, volley

Warm the bench, wave, whiff, whole new ballgame, windsurf, windup, wishbone

Zebra

III - 23
Word Parts - Geographic

Bay, bridge, brook, butte

City, country, creek

Dale, dell

East, estate

Fall, farm, farms, field, ford, forest

Garden, glen, green, grove

Haven, heights, high, highlands, hill, hills, house

Lake, land, ledge, long

Meadow, mesa, mill, mount, mountain

New, north

Old

Park, port, prairie

Ranch, ridge, rise, river, run

Shire, shores, south, spring, summer

Town

Valley, view, village

Way, west, winter, wood

III - 24
Logoworthy

Here is a short list of words that have two naming pluses: they are understood at a glance and they represent objects capable of depiction in simple drawings or silhouettes.

Ace, acorn, anchor, apple, arc, arch, arrow

Ball, bear, bird, bow, bridge

Cactus, cameo, cannon, carnation, castle, cat, circle, club, coin, colt, compass, crest, cross, crow, crown, cube

Deer, derby, diamond, domino, drum

Eagle, eye

Falcon, fan, flag, fox

Giant, gold medal, gorilla, gull

Hand, harp, hat, hawk, heart, helix, horizon, horn, horse

Ivy

Key

Ladybug, lamb, lattice, leaf, lighthouse, lily, lion

Magnet, mark, moon

Nautilus, nickel, nugget

Oak, orb, owl

Palm, peak, Pegasus, pelican, pentagon, plaid, plus, prism, pyramid

Quadrant

Rainbow, rose

Sail, sentry, shell, ship, silo, spur, square, star, sun, sunburst, sundial, sunflower, swan, sword

Talon, target, tiara, tomahawk, top hat, tree, triangle, trident

Umbrella

Volcano

Wave, weathervane, windmill, wolf

III - 25
Designators and Terminal Words

These words are attached to the end (usually) of a trade name to tell the world it is a business—sometimes in a very general way, sometimes specific. Some of these are legal terms and cannot be used unless true. You cannot call your outfit "Corporation" unless it is actually incorporated and registered in the state or states you do business in. "Company" is a broader word. In most states, it may designate either an incorporated or unincorporated business. Use of "Partnership" or "Cooperative" means the entity is a legal partnership or cooperative.

Alliance, and Daughters, and Sons, Associates, Assoc., Association, Assn.

Brokerage, Brokers, Business, Bureau

Center, Club, Coalition, Combine, Commerce, Commercial, Company, Co., Concern, Confederation, Conglomorate, Consortium, Co-op, Cooperative, Corp., Corporation, Crew

Department, Dept.

Emporium, Endeavor, Enterprise, Establishment

Factors, Factory, Family, Firm, Forum, Friends

Group, Guild

Holdings, House

Incorporated, Inc., Industries, Investments, Investors

Limited, Ltd.

Management, Merchant

Office, Operation, Organization

Partners, Partnership, Productions, Proprietorship, Proprietor, Prop.

Resources

Services, Shares, Society, Syndicate

Team

Union, United, Unity

Venture

Works

III - 26
Enduring Trademarks and Trade Names

1796 - Old Grand-Dad. Revived 1882

1818 - Brooks Brothers
1835 - Old Crow whiskey (Dr. James Crow)
1836 - Patent Arms Co. (Samuel Colt)
1837 - John Deere farm implements
1837 - Proctor & Gamble
1851 - Fruit of the Loom fabrics
1852 - Wells Fargo (later Railway Express Agency)
1857 - Jack Daniel's whiskey
1859 - The Great Atlantic & Pacific Tea Company
1859 - Vaseline
1862 - Chase & Sanborn coffee
1868 - Underwood's Deviled Ham
1869 - H. J. Heinz Company
1870 - Sherwin-Williams & Company
1872 - Phillips' Milk of Magnesia
1872 - Smith Brothers cough drops
1873 - Coors beer
1876 - Bell Telephone Company (AT&T)
1876 - Hires root beer
1877 - Quaker Oats
1878 - Mennen toiletries
1879 - Ivory soap
1881 - Twenty Mule Team Borax
1885 - French's mustard
1886 - Bon Ami polishing cleanser
1886 - Snake Oil liniment
1886 - Coca-Cola
1889 - Aunt Jemima pancakes
1893 - Cracker Jack snack

1893 - Cream of Wheat
1893 - Shredded Wheat
1896 - Tootsie Roll
1897 - Campbell's soup
1899 - Beech-Nut candy and gum
1899 - Buick Motor Company

1900 - Mack trucks
1903 - Ford Motor Company
1903 - Gillette blades
1904 - Buster Brown shoes
1912 - OREO cookies
1915 - Safeway Stores
1918 - Pepto-Bismol
1920 - Band-Aid

III - 27
Niche Name Hall of Fame

Anyone interested in business names is bound to have a list of all-time favorites. Here are some of mine:

Altoids, "The original, celebrated, curiously strong peppermints." Great names last, if the product is good too. Altoids, the box tells us, has been around since 1780.

Atchison, Topeka and Santa Fe Railroad, 1868.

Audubon Bird Call. A wooden plug inserted into a metal sleeve that is turned to create a bird-call sound. To the person in the street, John James Audubon is *the* name associated with birds, thus the appropriate knee-jerk link. They named the National Audubon Society after him, didn't they? The fact that Audubon shot the birds he painted instead of calling them is another matter.

Big Bertha. The first Big Bertha was a giant cannon, mounted on a railroad car, used by the Germans in World War I. It was named for Bertha Krupp, wife of Gustav Krupp, the munitions and armaments maker. This catchy, alliterative name has passed into the vernacular, like the Red Baron of the same vintage, and is now selling, of all things, golf clubs.

CadZZilla. Names a custom Cadillac made for a member of the ZZ Top rock band.

Cheers bar and television show. Can you top this?

Chris-Craft. The name (and the boats) were magic for me as a kid. Chris (from builder Chris Smith) and Craft, a serendipitous, alliterative name that to me, and millions of others, was, and is, synonymous with fun, panache, and speed over water.

Egghead Software. Clever beyond belief.

Garden Weasel. A garden cultivating tool. The fact that the weasel is not of the class of noble animals—weasel word, weasel out of the deal—commonly used to name things doesn't seem to matter. But the weasel animal is aggressive, and, I guess, the Garden Weasel goes after weeds aggressively. The name makes it stand out from the hundreds of unimaginatively named, or unnamed, garden tools in the store. It must work, because Garden Weasel has been around a long time and the label contains an impressive list of patents around the world.

Hooked on Phonics. Play on "hooked" and unforgettable telephone number, (800)-ABCDEFG.

Inc. magazine. The Power of Three (little letters).

Jaws. Best book and movie title ever? I must confess to liking one-word, this-says-it-all names.

Lego. Children's building blocks, said to be the most popular toy in the world. *Lego* is Latin for "to collect, select, pick out." What is the first word children speak: Mama, Papa, or Lego? The ultimate accolade.

Lookout Moon Pie. A marshmallow, chocolate, and cookie sandwich concoction, popular in the South since 1917. Moon Pies have been the butt of many jokes, but they just keep on selling.

Louisville Slugger baseball bats. An emotion-laden name, linked forever with the game. Kids do not want to be hitters of the ball, they dream of being sluggers, going for the fences.

Mad Coyote Salsa Mix. Tongue-in-cheek humor helps this astute Arizona company carve out a solid niche.

NeXT Computers. A masterpiece.

Oil Can Henry's. Quick oil change shops. With a glut of me-too, sound-alike competitors' names, this one stands out. It is a blend of clever personification (Oil Can was a cartoon character) and a throw-back to small-town America—neighborhood garages with oil-soaked, wooden floors, hand-pumped gasoline, and guys hanging around talking cars.

The Original Pancake House. I like the word *original* in a name, if it is honest. This Portland, Oregon, restaurant, franchised around the country, was founded in the 1950s and may actually be the first to serve a breakfast-only menu. Other *Original* favorites: Original Mink Oil (boot and shoe waterproofing compound), and the Original American Kazoo Company of Eden, New York.

Pierce-Arrow and Stanley Steamer. These would be my favorite old-time automobile names: Pierce-Arrow because of its mellow sound, suggestive "straight as," and play on *pierce*. Stanley Steamer for balance and stick-in-the-mind alliteration.

Sun Valley. Ketchum, Idaho, is one of America's most desirable places to live and play. But it got that way as Sun Valley (and a little help from Mt. Baldy and W. Averell Harriman). The name was the creation of snow-hating public-relations man Steve Hannagan in the 1930s.

U-Haul. One-way trailer and truck rentals. If this is not my all-time favorite commercial name, it is close. It has everything: one word, passes all the basic tests, stylistic "you," and excellent readability going down the road, stating what it is all about, clearly, concisely, and distinctly.

Waldorf-Astoria Hotel. Waldorf was the town in Germany where New York City merchant-king John Jacob Astor grew up. Astoria, the trading post on the Columbia River, 1811, was his most notable venture, immortalized in Washington Irving's book of that name. The original New York hotel was a joining of the Waldorf and the Astoria, each built by different factions of the Astor family. The final name is a perfect fit, with a two syllable–four syllable cadence, connoting elegance and sophistication.

Water Music. This names a houseboat, and a more beautiful and appropriate name I could not imagine. My favorite sailboat name, by the way, is *Paradocs.* Both were found in Seattle, which figures, since it is a huge boating center. Favorite motorboat name: *Cirrhosis of the River*, a fictional boat that plied the Ohio River in a work I unfortunately cannot remember.

Honorable mention:

Apple Computers. Clearly a breakthrough name.

Black Inc. For an investment club, among other things.

King Kelly marmalade. (Michael Joseph "King" Kelly, ballplayer?)

Lotus 1-2-3 spreadsheet program. Heir to VisiCalc. High technology made simple as one, two, three.

Snickers candy bars. A friendly, light-hearted name for an impulse item. A close call, because all the candies that have survived very long have great names—Butterfinger, Almond Joy, Baby Ruth, M&Ms, Mars, etc.

Windows on the World. The restaurant atop the World Trade Center in New York City. Also in New York, oxymoronish Cellar in the Sky. I have never been to them, but they must be good, because they have such great names.

WordPerfect. Preemptive.

III - 28
Commonly Used Trade Names

This list is taken from a marketing directory for metropolitan Portland, Oregon. It is easily adaptable for your use, wherever you live. (Portland is often used in market surveys as a "typical" American city.) For the locally and regionally popular words found here, such as West Coast, Columbia, Northwest, just substitute equivalent ones for your area—Southeast, Missouri, Rocky Mountain, etc. The rankings should be approximately the same.

Here we have the classic naming dilemma. Do we adopt a name because it is popular? Or is that the precise reason to shun it? If popular, it must work, or so conventional wisdom would have it. Or is it popular because so many business owners gave so little thought to the naming process in the first place—just went along with the crowd? Is it to your advantage or disadvantage to become one of hundreds of Northwest (or Northeast, Southeast, Southwest, Midwest) This or That Companies? The higher up the list, the more the word is in everyday usage, thus presumably passing the basic tests. The farther down, the more "distinctive," possibly passing different tests, but perhaps having a tougher time with the basics. Note: The truly distinctive trade names found in the Portland area do not appear on this list at all.

961 - Regional designation (470 - Northwest; 230 - Western; 197 - West [including local compass, meaning west side of town]; 50 - West Coast; 14 - Far West)

583 - State name (Oregon)

460 - City name (Portland)

310 - Geographic - ocean (Pacific)

287 - America or American
233 - Geographic - major river (Columbia)

194 - United (140 - Uni, United; 27 - Unified; 27 - Union)
190 - Sun (110 - Sun and Sunny, 50 - Sunset, 30 - Sunshine)
170 - Geographic - mountain range (Cascade)
138 - Local compass - (North)
132 - Pro, Professional
131 - Local compass - (East, Eastside, Eastgate, Eastern, etc.)
110 - Geographic - major river (Willamette)

95 - All
92 - Local compass - (South)
91 - Tri, Triple

85 - Gold, Golden
83 - Custom

79 - Country
78 - New
76 - National
75 - International
73 - King
70 - U.S.

69 - First
63 - Metro
63 - Quality
62 - Advance, Advanced
60 - Regional popular (Evergreen)

59 - Design, Designers, Designs
57 - Associated
55 - City
55 - Classic
55 - Industrial
55 - City nicknames (Rose City, Rip City, River City)
55 - Pioneer

55 - Royal
55 - Valley
54 - General
53 - Park
51 - Business
50 - Great
50 - Old, Olde

48 - Commercial
46 - Action
45 - Creative
45 - Technical, Tech, Technical, Technology, Tek
43 - Best
42 - House of
41 - Crown
40 - A-1
40 - Quick, Quik
40 - Red, Red's

39 - Bob's
39 - Village
38 - Continental
37 - Community
36 - Allied
36 - Alpine
36 - Special, Specialized, Specialty
36 - Superior
35 - Executive
35 - Master
35 - Town, Towne, Town & Country
35 - Universal
34 - Sport, Sports, Sportsman
33 - Central
32 - Alpha
31 - Interstate
30 - Micro

28 - ABC

28 - Ace
28 - Consolidated
28 - Perfect
28 - Standard
28 - Super
27 - Family
27 - Imperial
26 - Top
25 - Eagle
25 - Metropolitan
24 - AAA
24 - Reliable
24 - Grand
24 - One
23 - Budget
21 - Magic
21 - Star
21 - Total
20 - Apollo
20 - Arrow
20 - Diamond
20 - Independent
20 - Safe
20 - Speed, Speedy

19 - Center
19 - Delta
19 - Horizon
18 - Atlas
18 - Image
18 - Original
18 - Service
18 - Your
17 - Able
17 - Unique
16 - Brass
16 - Economy
16 - Good

16 - My
16 - Acme
15 - Lincoln
15 - Omni
15 - Viking
14 - Champion
14 - Discount
14 - Modern
14 - Plaza
14 - Security
14 - Trade
13 - Performance
13 - Miracle
13 - Natural
12 - Complete
11 - Ideal
11 - Just
11 - Progressive
11 - Vista
10 - Prime
10 - Value
10 - Vintage

9 - Cornerstone
9 - Guardian
9 - Mutual
8 - Prince, Princess
8 - Guarantee
8 - Minute, Minit
8 - Shamrock
7 - Express
7 - Omega
6 - Easy
6 - Genuine
6 - Pyramid
3 - Beta
2 - Republic

PART IV - APPENDIX

IV - 1
Glossary

Acronym: A word formed from the initial letters of a name, such as NATO, for North Atlantic Treaty Alliance, or by combining initial letters or parts of a series of words, such as radar, from radio detecting and ranging.

Alliteration: Two words having the same initial sound. Winter wind, Wonder Woman, Mighty Mite.

Argot: A specialized vocabulary or set of idioms used by a particular class or group.

Assonance: Resemblance in sound. A partial rhyme in the vowel sounds. Brave and vain.

Assumed business name: A trade name.

Brand name: A trademark.

Coined mark: A mark that has no meaning and is created solely for use as a trademark.

Collective mark: A trademark or service mark used by members of a group or organization.

Common law trademark: Unregistered trademarks protected by court-made law, as opposed to statutory law.

Composite mark: A trademark consisting of words or parts of words. Referred to in text as combination names.

Consonance: Correspondence or harmony of sounds. Repetition of terminal consonants. Rain and tone.

Copyright: Protection to authors of original works, including literary, dramatic, musical, artistic, and other intellectual works. Administered by the Copyright Office of the Library of Congress, Washington, D.C. 20599.

Corporate name: The name of a corporation, as registered with the state granting its charter or other states in which it does business.

d.b.a.: Abbreviation for "doing business as." Sally Smith, d.b.a. Sally's Floral Design.

Descriptive mark: A mark that communicates information about the product or service. Speedy Towing Service.

Designation: A distinguishing name or title, such as Corporation or Company.

Dissonance: A harsh or disagreeable combination of sounds.

Distinctive mark: A mark that can be associated by relevant members of the public and trade with its source.

Eponym: The name of something derived from the name of a person. Macadamia nut, after John Macadam, or macintosh raincoat, after Charles Macintosh.

Etymology: The origin and history of a word as it comes into present usage.

Euphemism: The substitution of an inoffensive word or phrase for one considered offensive. To "pass away" in place of "to die."

Fictitious business name: An assumed business name or alias.

Generic word: Descriptive of an entire group or class.

Idiom: An expression that cannot be understood from the individual meanings of its words. Pass the buck, high and dry.

Lanham Act, or Federal Trademark Act of 1946: Provides for registration of marks used "in commerce," and additional remedies for owners of unregistered trademarks under the theory of unfair competition.

Logo: From logogram and logotype. A unique, symbolic representation of a name.

Mark: A trademark, service mark, certification mark, or collective mark.

Metaphor: A figure of speech in which a term is transferred from the object it normally describes to an object designated by implicit comparison or analogy. Evening of life.

Mnemonic: The ability to trigger meaningfulness to the user. Assisting the memory. A formula or rhyme used as an aid to remembering. Thirty days hath September....

Morpheme: A meaningful word or word part that cannot be divided into smaller meaningful parts. Man, bad.

Name: A word or words by which an entity is designated and distinguished from others. Synonyms: Alias, handle, moniker, nickname, pen name, pseudonym, sobriquet.

Neologism: A newly coined word or expression.

Onomatopoeia: The formation of words that imitate what they denote. Ooze, murmur, buzz, quack, drip.

Oxymoron: A rhetorical figure of speech in which incongruous or contradictory terms are combined. Deafening silence, mournful optimist, instant tradition.

Patent: A grant made by a government giving the creator of an invention the sole right to make, use, and sell that invention for a set period of time.

Proprietary name: Exclusively owned, private.

Pun: A play on words, sometimes on different senses of the same word, and sometimes on the similar sense or sound of different words.

Service mark: Any word, name, symbol, device, or combination of them used to identify and distinguish the services of one person or organization from those of another.

Simile: A figure of speech in which two essentially unlike things are compared, often in a phrase introduced by *like* or *as*. He was strong as a bull.

Slogan: An advertising phrase expressing something about a business, product, or service.

Sonorous: A full, rich, or deep sound.

Surname: Family name.

Trade dress: The elements used in presentation of a product or service, such as name, color, logo, packaging, etc. The total effect.

Trademark: A word, phrase, design, slogan, or symbol that identifies a specific product.

Trademark notice: A notice used with a mark to indicate that it is federally registered (®), or that it is registered with a state or common-law rights are claimed (™ or ™).

Trade name: A name used to identify a business or vocation.

IV - 2
Helpful Reading

Bayan, Richard. *Words That Sell.* Chicago: Contemporary Books, Inc., 1986.

> This book contains list after list of power words, primarily for creating advertising copy, but useful in naming, too.

Charmasson, Henri. *The Name Is the Game: How to Name a Company or Product.* Homewood, IL: Dow Jones-Irwin, 1988.

> An outstanding book by a principal in a naming firm. For those wishing to delve further into the process of business name creation. It is a scholarly work, however, which some readers may find a bit overwhelming.

Everyone's Guide to Copyrights, Trademarks, and Patents. The Comprehensive Handbook for Protecting Your Writing, Inventions, and Other Creative Work. With Official, Ready-to-Use Applications Forms. Philadelphia: Running Press, 1990.

> An easy-to-read, 176-page book, *Everyone's* compiles excerpts from informational publications of the U.S. Copyright Office and the U.S. Patent and Trademark Office.

McGrath, Kate and Stephen Elias. *Trademark:How to Name a Business & Product.* Berkeley: Nolo Press, 1992.

> The emphasis in this clearly written book is on the legalities of trademarks. Here is how the book describes itself on the cover: "A Friendly Guide to the Laws that Govern Commercial Names. Especially designed for small business, this book shows how to: choose a name competitors can't copy, conduct a trademark search, and know your rights if there is

a dispute over the use of a trademark. Includes all official forms & instructions necessary to register with the U.S. Patent & Trademark Office."

Miller, Arthur R. *Intellectual Property: Patents, Trademarks and Copyright in a Nutshell.* St. Paul: West Publishing Co., 1983.

An overview book for lawyers, heavy on citations of legal cases recounting past trademark battles, and light on practical help for namesmiths. A good starter text, if that is your area of interest.

Morgan, Hal. *Symbols of America: A Lavish Celebration of America's Best-Loved Trademarks and the Products They Symbolize— Their History, Folklore, and Enduring Mystique.* New York: Viking Penguin, Inc., 1986.

Murphy, John M. *Branding: A Key Marketing Tool.* New York: McGraw-Hill Book Company, 1987.

Originally published in England, *Branding* is a collection of essays by experts in the field. My favorites: "What is Branding" and "Developing New Brand Names," John M. Murphy; "The History of Branding," Adrian Room; "The Psychology of Names," Leslie Collins; "The Branding of Services," Russell Taylor; "The Wide World of Branding," Terry Oliver.

Ries, Al, and Jack Trout. *Positioning: The Battle for Your Mind.* New York: Warner Books, 1981.

This is one of the few marketing or advertising books I have found that gives more than passing mention to business names, let alone good counsel on how to create them. (Most cover the subject in one or two paragraphs, sometimes offering very simplistic, in my opinion, if not downright misleading advice—thus one of the reasons for *Names That Sell.*) The authors are renowned marketing gurus who express themselves powerfully in print.

To whet your appetite for this marketing classic—what a knockout title!—let me quote the pertinent chapter and heading titles:

"Chapter 9, The Power of the Name. How to choose a name. How not to choose a name. When to use a coined name. Negative names can be positive. Bringing the product out of the closet. David and Michael and Hubert and Elmer. Hubert and Elmer in the sky. The Akron twins. The Toledo triplets. Continental confusion.

"Chapter 10, The No-Name Trap. [This chapter deals mainly with the folly of using initials as names.] Phonetic shorthand. Visual shorthand. No shortcuts to success. The mind works by ear. Name obsolescence. The confusion between cause and effect. Acronyms and phone directories."

Spears, Richard A. *NTC's American Idioms Dictionary.* Lincolnwood, IL: National Textbook Company, 1975.

There are, of course, endless volumes of word and phrase compilations for namesmiths to explore — limited only by the depth of your favorite library or bookstore.

Weinstein, David A. *How to Protect Your Business, Professional, and Brand Names.* New York: John Wiley & Sons, Inc., 1990.

Mr. Weinstein is a trademark attorney. His 294-page book, in addition to discussing the words that make up trademarks, touches on color, shape, design, etc. He goes into detail about the various degrees of distinctiveness and how marks can become distinctive. A helpful chapter deals with searches. In addition, he instructs the reader in state and federal registration procedures.

IV - 3
Index

Do you need help with your naming?

Name Review Service. Send us your top name candidates or names in use. We reply with a written opinion and suggestions. One flat rate. Inexpensive. Quick response. Wherever you live, if you have a telephone number or mailing address, we can help. Write, call, or fax for information on this and other naming products and services.

Alder Press
P.O. Box 1503
Portland, OR 97207
Phone: (503) 246-7983
Fax: (503) 452-4265

To order *Names That Sell:*

Mail: Send a check for $14.95 per copy, plus $2.55 shipping and handling, total $17.50, to Alder Press. Please do not send cash. Include your name, address, city, state, ZIP code, phone number, and the book title. Satisfaction guaranteed, or your money back.

Telephone: Credit card users may order toll-free, 24 hours, seven days a week. Call Publishers Group, (800) 858-9055.

Multiple copies: To order copies in quantity or for resale, write, call, or fax for information.

We would like to hear from you.

Your comments and suggestions are always appreciated.